SAT Ⅱ :
Writing with Essay Workbook

- 미국에서 배우는 영어 문법과 작문 -

Written by KiHoon Pyo
JiSun Lee

HAKMUN PUBLISHING CO.

Preface

책을 발간하며 …

1989년 한국의 한 평범한 고등학생이었던 저는 미국으로 유학을 떠나게 되었습니다. 당시 대부분의 학생들이 그러하였듯, 영어교육의 절대적인 지침서로 인식되었던 성문종합영어를 수차례 학습하였고, 문법에서만은 자신이 있다고 생각했었습니다. 하지만 미국 고등학교 입학과 동시에 한국에서의 영어교육이 얼마나 잘못되는지를 느끼게 되었습니다. 한국에서 받은 영어교육은 단순한 문장의 기계적인 해석은 가능하게 하였지만 실제로 표현하고자 하는 영작문은 머리 속에서 한국어로 맴돌 뿐 한 문단을 채울 수가 없었습니다. 그로부터 14년이 지나 한국에 귀국한 저는 대형서점에 가보았습니다. 14년 전 성문종합영어에 국한되있던 영문법에 관한 서적이 다양화된 것을 발견할 수 있었습니만 아무리 훑어보아도 '과연 이 책들의 내용으로 영작력을 향상시킬 수 있을까' 라는 강한 의구심을 갖게 되었습니다.

한국의 대학수학능력시험에 해당되는 미국대학입학시험인 SAT(Scholastic Assessment Test)는 SAT I과 SAT II(Subject Test), 두 종류로 양분됩니다. SAT II 중에서도 가장 중요시되는 SAT II의 작문(Writing)은, 미국에서 쓰여지는 가장 핵심적인 문법을 영작과 연관시켜 능력을 평가하는 것으로 학생에게 영문법과 영작을 함께 이해하여 옳은 문장을 만들어내도록 요구하고 있습니다. 단순한 문법의 오류를 찾아내는 문제에서부터 문법상에는 오류가 없지만 문장을 새로 구성함으로써 표현하고자 하는 의미를 향상시키는 능력을 테스트하는 문제들로 구성되어 있습니다.

이 책은 SAT II Writing(작문) 시험을 준비하는 유학생들에게는 기본적인 안내와 핵심 문법 리뷰 등의 제공을 통하여 효율적인 시험대비에 도움이 되고자 하며, 국내 학생들에게는 기존의 낡은 문법의 그늘에서 탈피, 현재 미국에서 통용되는 영문법을 접하게 하고 핵심적인 토픽 리뷰 및 영작과 문법을 함께 연계하여 공부하는 새로운 학습법을 제시하여 효과적인 영어문법학습에 도움이 되고자 합니다.

미국 현지에서 유학생, 교포, 그리고 미국인들에 이르기까지 문법과 작문(Grammar/Writing)을 10년간 지도해오면서 얻은 소중한 현장 지식과 경험을 바탕으로 이 책은 쓰여졌습니다. 끝으로 이 책을 저와 함께 만드신 이지선 선생님, 그리고 다양한 영어학습 정보를 주신 박현자 어학원 원장님과 서울대학교 입학관리본부 주현준 전문위원님께 감사의 말씀을 드립니다.

2003년 4월 대치동 연구실에서

저자 표기훈

Contents

Part I

Part II

Appendix

Part

1

SAT II : Writing with Essay Workbook

SAT II : Writing with Essay Workbook

SAT II : Writing with Essay Workbook

SAT II : Writing with Essay Workbook

SAT II : Writing with Essay Workbook

SAT II : Writing with Essay Workbook

SAT II : Writing with Essay Workbook

SAT II : Writing with Essay Workbook

SAT II : Writing with Essay Workbook

SAT II : Writing with Essay Workbook

SAT II : Writing with Essay Workbook

SAT II : Writing with Essay Workbook

SAT II : Writing with Essay Workbook

SAT II : Writing with Essay Workbook

Chapter 1

SUBJECT-VERB AGREEMENT

 Subject-Verb Agreement: the 12 Commandments

The fundamental rule for subject-verb agreement is that a subject must agree with its verb in number; that is, a singular subject (one thing or unit idea) requires a singular verb, whereas a plural subject (more than one) needs a plural verb.

Singular

> - <u>Paul</u> *needs* a date for the dance.
> - <u>The tree</u> *grows* in the bright sunlight.
> - <u>A boy</u> whom I met in school *is named* Tony.

Plural

> - <u>Paul and his sister</u> *need* dates for the dance.
> - <u>The tree and the flowers</u> *grow* in the bright sunlight.
> - <u>The boys</u> whom I met in school *are named* Tony and Tommy.

All sentences like the ones above are straightforward, *and* they rarely confuse people.

Commandment 1 | Compound Subjects Linked by "And"

A compound subject is more than one subject. These subjects are joined by *and*. In all cases they need a plural verb.

> • <u>Troublemakers</u> and <u>bad situations</u> *seem* to go together.
> • <u>A new idea</u> and <u>a bored boy</u> *equal* trouble.
> • <u>The boy</u> and <u>his cats</u> *live* in the playhouse.

Commandment 2 | Compound Subjects Linked by "Or"

When two subjects are linked by the word *or*, the verb can be singular or plural. The verb should agree with the subject closest to the *or*, regardless of whether the other subject is singular or plural.

> • A brother or <u>a sister</u> *is* fun to have as a sibling.
> • *Are* <u>tickets</u> or passes required for admission into the concert?
> • Either the grandparents or <u>the mother</u> *picks* up the child.
> • The principal or <u>the teachers</u> *punish* the students.

Commandment 3 | Compound Subjects Linked by "Neither ... nor" or "Either ... or"

In the cases of *neither ... nor* and *either ... or*, the verb should agree with the second subject, the one that follows *nor* or *or*.

> - Either the goats or the <u>cow</u> *munches* grass.
> - Neither the boys nor <u>Jane</u> *likes* vegetables.
> - Either the farmer or the <u>cowboys</u> *love* to knit.
> - Neither Joe nor the <u>students</u> *enjoy* writing class.

Commandment 4 | Subjects That Are Always Singular

Some subjects are always singular. These subjects are:

🔒 the **every~** words (**everybody, everyone**)

> - <u>Every</u> dog and cat *is* registered in the animal shelter.
> - <u>Everybody</u> *enjoys* vacations.
> - <u>Everyone</u> is *going* to the party.

🔒 the **any~** words (**anybody, anyone**)

> - <u>Any can</u> on the shelf *is* fine.
> - <u>Anybody</u> who goes bungee-jumping *is* crazy.
> - <u>Anyone</u> remaining in the contest *deserves* a prize.

🔒 the **no~** words (**nobody, no one**)

> - <u>Nobody</u> in the applicant pool *is* qualified for the job.
> - <u>No one</u> I called *has returned* my message.

Subjects that are preceded by *either*, *neither*, or *many a* are singular.

> • <u>Either</u> of the girls *is going* to the supermarket.
> • <u>Neither</u> of the two *has done* the homework.
> • <u>Many a</u> college graduate *has* found himself wishing to return to freshman year.

Subjects that preceded by *each* is singular.

> • <u>Each</u> of the children *is going* to try to hit the piñata.

Commandment 5 | Subjects with Predicate Nouns of Different Number

A predicate noun renames the subject. In the sentence, *Jane is our president*, Jane and president mean the same person. Don't get confused when the subject and predicate noun are different in number. The verb must still agree with the subject.

> • The <u>prize</u> *was* three brand new fiction books.
> • The best <u>gift</u> for him *is* hermit crabs for his collection.
> • <u>Hermit crabs</u> *are* the best and most appreciated gift for him.

Commandment 6 | Nouns That Sound Plural But Are Singular

Such nouns are those that end in "s" but are singular, such as *news*, *measles*, *mumps*, *molasses*, *economics*, *mathematics*, *politics*, *physics*, etc.

> • <u>Economics</u> *makes* my head hurt.
> • <u>Mumps</u> *is* a highly contagious.

However, nouns that come "in pairs" take a plural verb, such as *scissors, binoculars, pants, trousers, glasses,* etc.

> • Where *are* my <u>glasses</u>?

Commandment 7 | Subjects That Are Collective Nouns

Collective nouns are those that describe a group of individual items, such as *family, jury,* and *team.* When the meaning of the sentence implies that the noun is acting as one group, the collective subject takes a singular verb.

> • The <u>jury</u> *hands* in its verdict today.
> • The <u>family</u> *eats* together in the dining room.
> • The <u>team</u> *wins* the championship by a nose.

When the meaning of the sentence emphasizes the individual parts of the group, and the noun is not acting as one group, the collective subject takes a plural verb.

> • The <u>jury</u> *have* been exchanging their opinions for over an hour.
> • The <u>family</u> *were* arguing about where to go for vacation.
> • The <u>team</u> *were* discussing various strategies with each other.

Commandment 8 | Sentences Starting with "There," "Here" or "Where"

These words may start a sentence but they will never be the subjects of a sentence. The verb following these words must agree with the subject which is found somewhere after the verb.

> - There *are* <u>speechs</u> we have to write.
> - Here *is* <u>the magazine</u> you requested.
> - Where *do* these <u>books</u> go?

Commandment 9 | Indefinite Constructions

These sentences are those that start with the word *"it"* followed by a conjugated form of the *"to be"* verb.

> - <u>It is</u> a rainy day.
> - <u>It was</u> I who said that it would rain.
> - <u>It was</u> the children who played with the garbage.

Note how the verb after *"it"* is always singular, no matter what the subject is.

Commandment 10 | "A Number" versus "The Number"

This is a simple one to remember. When the subject is a number, the verb is plural, since the number can be many numbers. When the subject is the number, the verb is singular, since the number can only be one number.

> • <u>A number of</u> children *are* going to the park.
> • <u>The number of</u> children going to the park *is* limited to five.

C *ommandment 11* | Relative Pronouns

When a relative pronoun (who, which, that) immediately precedes a verb, that verb must agree with the noun immediately in front of the relative pronoun.

> • Jewel is *one of the children* who ...

the verb that follows will agree with the noun in front of the relative pronoun who:

> • Jewel is *one of the <u>children</u> who <u>sing</u>* jazz.

The verb is plural because the sentence indicates that many children sing jazz, and that Jane is merely one of them.

However, if you have the word "only" involved,

> • Jewel is the *<u>only</u> one of the children who* ...

the verb that follows will be singular:

> • Jewel is the *only one of the children who <u>sings</u>* jazz.

C *ommandment 12* | Prepositional Phrases

Watch out for intervening phrases or clauses between the subject and verb that disguise the subject. Often these phrases are *prepositional phrases*.

> • The bustling <u>activity</u> (of many bees) *hums* in the meadows.
> • The <u>announcement</u> (in the school newspaper) (by the reporters) (who covered the PTA meetings) *reveals* that those meetings were well attended.

Hmmm, but what are prepositional phrases?

A preposition is a word that conveys position, direction, time or other abstraction by relating its object to another sentence element.

A prepositional phrase is made up of a preposition, its object, and any modifiers of the object.

> • The symphony is by the greatest Korean musician.

In this sentence the prepositional phrase is *by the greatest Korean musician.* The preposition is *by*, the object is *musician*, and the modifiers *are the greatest Korean.*

Identifying prepositional phrases is important in figuring out subject-verb agreement in a sentence, for the prepositional phrases often come between the subject and verb and masks the agreement.

> • The comments in the article *is* valid.

At first glance, the subject-verb agreement seems correct because of the prepositional phrase that precedes the verb.

> • The comments ~~in the article~~ *are* valid.

Removing the prepositional phrase makes subject-verb agreement clear.

List of Common Prepositions

aboard	between	in case of	over
about	beyond	in front of	past
above	by	in place of	pending
according to	by means of	in regard to	regardless of
across	by way of	in spite of	regarding
after	concerning	including	since
against	despite	inside	through
along	down	instead of	throughout
along with	due to	into	till
among	during	like	to
apart from	except	near	toward
around	except for	next to	under
as	excluding	of	underneath
as for	for	off	unlike
aside from	from	on	until
at	from across	on account of	unto
because of	from between	on behalf of	up
before	from under	on top of	upon
behind	in	onto	with
below	in accordance with	out	with regard to
beneath	in addition to	out of	within
beside	in back of	outside	without

Remember, an infinitive (to followed by the basic form of a verb) is a verbal, not a prepositional phrase.

Identifying Prepositional Phrases

 Underline the prepositions in the sentences below.

1. Trention is the capital of New Jersey.

2. Paul's book is about a young girl and her dog.

3. I walked past Tony's house every evening last week.

4. California is a state on the west coast.

5. Adolescents are approximately between the age of 12 and 18.

6. Superman's eyes can detect cracks in metal.

7. When I am really tired, I feel as if I can sleep for 100 years.

8. Our bodies are mostly composed of water.

9. Trees have been made into paper, pencils, and other various products.

10. The young boy has a cast on his arm.

Prepositional Phrases

Underline the prepositional phrases in the sentences below.

1. One of the items on display at the store was a picture of one of the U.S. Presidents.

2. The pitcher can throw a ball at 99 miles per hour.

3. Holding the box under her arm, Patty attempted to open the door with her other hand.

4. A refrigerator should be kept at thirty-seven degrees and a freezer at zero.

5. The permeability of the gauze pads on adhesive bandages help air circulate around wounds.

6. I was born on a small farm in Korea in 1977.

7. During World War I observatory balloons were used to watch for submarines.

8. The Shinto religion is very much concerned with human interaction with nature.

9. Seoul is the capital of Korea.

10. In 1492, Columbus discovered the Americas while on a search for the spices of the Indies.

11. I'll meet you in front of school in the morning.

12. Americans continue to choose junk food as their favorite snacks in spite of repeated warnings against eating too much fat.

13. I plan to drop out of school regardless of my teachers' objections.

14. On a small island in the Pacific, there is a single palm tree that grows nuggets of gold.

15. Please leave the hot pepper out of the soup.

Subject–Verb Agreement Exercise 1

Correct any errors in subject-verb agreement.

1. At the end of the season, the TV couple, regardless of their ratings, are splitting up.

2. The article that told the story of thirty young people who died in an overly enthusiastic mosh pit were gripping to read.

3. Either Bush or Gore is going to win the election.

4. Before they were laid off by the academy, neither the verbal teachers nor Jerry the math teacher were told that their jobs were in danger.

5. Jerry's talent in EverQuest and badminton, one of our school's most popular activities, prove his often questioned mental and physical strength.

6. Charles Darwin, along with his contemporary Sigmund Freud, are among the most revolutionary scientific figures in nineteenth century history.

7. Jeanie, along with her friend Ellen, appear to be running down the street.

8. Here's the two references to which the paper cites as irrefutable evidence for its claim.

9. The unpaved parts of the track, which runs four miles east from here, is only about two hundred yards long.

10. Joe Kang and Jay Kang, who began their landscaping business last summer, have decided to invest in a new lawn mower.

11. According to the noted historian Jisun Lee, there is rarely only one interpretation of any historical event that is universally accepted.

12. Despite numerous professed sightings, there is still no conclusive evidence of the alleged existence of Joe Park's brain.

13. Through the doors of the cathedral passes more than fifty people each day.

14. There were a number of congressmen debating Clinton's impeachment.

15. Both the word scuba and the word laser are acronyms.

16. Donations to the church-sponsored orphanage is up by 50 percent over last year.

17. In this film, there is only a semblance of a romance plot and an undisguised misogyny.

18. It is said that neither poor weather nor poor health keeps a postman from making his rounds.

19. The level of chemicals and other air pollutants is now monitored by environmental organizations such as the Environmental Protection Agency.

20. The coal industry, along with worker safety issues, are of great concern to the residents of West Virginia.

Subject–Verb Agreement Exercise 2

Choose the correct verb for each subject.

1. None of the people at the company (was, were) pleased with the results of the contest.

2. A few in my class (was, were) asked to stay after the bell.

3. The lack of funds (present, presents) a problem.

4. Some of these books (has, have) hand-painted illustrations.

5. Everybody living in Fort Lee (go, goes) to Fort Lee High School.

6. A band with two drummers and thirty-five oboes (sound, sounds) terrible.

7. One of my friends (play, plays) the trombone and hates it.

8. All of our stuff (is, are) packed in boxes in the attic.

9. Each of the children (was, were) having a great time.

10. Every one of these cars (is, are) too expensive.

Revise the following sentences according to the instructions that appear in brackets. Make sure the subject and verb of the new sentence agree.

11. Our team has made it to the championship tournament.

    [Add *Three members of* before *Our team*.]

12. Each of my colleagues was excited because of the proposed raise.

    [Change *Each* to *Many*.]

13. Has anybody quit the team?

    [Change *anybody* to *any of the boys*.]

14. The batter was disappointed in the referee's decision.

    [Add *as well as the other players* after *batter*. Set off the addition with commas.]

15. All of the fruit is rotten.

    [Change *fruit* to *pineapples*.]

16. Most of the classrooms were equipped with new computer monitors.

    [Change *Most* to *None*.]

17. The boss leaves tomorrow on the business trip to Florida.

    [Add *accompanied by three secretaries* after *class*. Set off the addition with commas.]

18. Every one of the chairs was broken.

    [Change *Every one* to *All but two*.]

19. Some of her suggestions have been approved.

    [Change *suggestions* to *plan*.]

20. Both of them usually do very well in school.

    [Change *Both of them* to *Everyone*.]

Subject–Verb Agreement Exercise 3

⚫ *Choose the correct verb for each subject.*

1. In subject-verb agreement, one must be wary of intervening phrases, such as this one, that (occludes, occlude) the true nature of agreement.

2. The lack of rhythm in his dance, in addition to the jerky movements that he imitates from real dancers, (causes, cause) people around him to laugh and move away in fear of association.

3. Did you know that enormous plates of rock (is, are) moving constantly beneath the earth's surface?

4. Heavy, unrelenting pressure placed against one's wrist contrary to the natural hinge motion of the elbow (forces, force) the elbow joint to break.

5. If the vision of that last sentence (is, are) disturbing, I apologize.

6. But the study of subject-verb agreement (is, are) not always a happy task and is in fact often grueling and painful.

7. The SAT II Writing test, as well as the other tests offered by ETS, (has, have) been shown to be predict one's level of academic achievement in college.

8. This correlation often cited by many educators in favor of standardized testing (is, are) considered to be the only justification for keeping a test that is otherwise regarded to be biased.

9. Many students in New Jersey, as well as those in other states across the country, (has, have) complained about this issue.

10. However, SAT academy businesses, most of which are clustered in Northern New Jersey, (is, are) in the fullest support of SAT testing.

🔵 *Correct for any errors in subject-verb agreement.*

1. Either of your ideas seems plausible.

2. Bullets for his gun is the most appropriate gift.

3. Some of the essay wasn't relevant.

4. The cause of the recent string of burglaries are being investigated.

5. That letter or the package goes to the office.

6. I think that his office is infested with insects.

7. Only a few on any committee do all the work.

8. Each of the games run on a different program.

9. It looks as though the pets have their fleas well under control.

10. The clown, as well as his clown friends, were in the parade.

11. None of the team members has disagreed with my directive.

12. Neither of the experiments follow the correct procedure.

13. The reason for absences have been justified.

14. Insun knows that the kind of problems his dogs had have been related to their diet.

15. Did the results of that study show that hamsters learn bad habits easily?

16. That student, as well as his teammates, has been the focus of more than one satirical report.

17. With luck every one of the students have passed the final exam.

18. Three weeks are a long time to worry about a meeting.

19. Paul, don't you think that six quarts is a lot of water?

20. Most of his lectures holds my interest.

Chapter 2

PRONOUN CASE

 Nominative/Subjective Case

These pronouns are: *I, he, she, we, they, you, (who)*

The nominative case is used to replace or refer to nouns that are subjects of the sentence, namely the nouns that are carrying out the verb's action in the sentence.

> • He will be going to the park tomorrow.
>
> • It was she who said that it would hail.
>
> • I am smarter than she (is).
>
> • Who shall I say is calling?

 ## Objective Case

These pronouns are: *me, him, her, us, them, you, (whom)*

The objective case is used to refer to nouns that do not carry out any action in the sentence. Most often these pronouns turn out to be objects of the preposition.

- The scandal should be kept a secret between *you* and *me*.
- This was given to *her* by *him*.
- To *whom* should I give this gift?

 ## Possessive Pronouns

These pronouns show ownership or possession:
my, mine, your, yours, his, hers, its, our, ours, theirs, whose

- This is *my* cookie.
- This is *your* doughnut.

Remember that if there is a pronoun right before a gerund, that pronoun must be possessive to show that the action belongs to that noun.

- *My* screaming scared the little girl.
- The most annoying thing about him is *his* whining.

A gerund is a word that ends in "-ing" that looks like a verb but is used in the sentence as a noun.

 ## Relative Pronouns

These pronouns refer to other nouns: *who, whom, that, which, whose* (*whoever, whomever, whichever, whatever*)

Who and *whom* refer to people; *that* and *which* to animals and objects; *whose* to people, animals and objects.

> - Anyone *who* wants to become a doctor must attend medical school.
> - The dog *that* ran away was later found.
> - The dog, *which* I once kicked, had run away but was later found.
> - *Whose* blanket is this?

 ## Reflexive and Intensive Pronouns

These are pronouns that add *-self* to the pronoun:
myself, yourself, himself, herself, itself, ourselves, yourselves, themselves

A reflexive pronoun refers back to the subject.

> - He hit *himself* by mistake.
> - I know *myself* best.

An intensive pronoun is used to intensify, or to clarify and emphasize.

> • She fixed the car herself.
> • I myself was the culprit.

 ## Tips on choosing the correct pronoun case

Commandment 1 | Use the nominative case when replacing or referring to the subject of the sentence.

> • He and *I* went to school.
> • The person who deserves the blame is *I*.

Commandment 2 | Use the objective case when the pronoun is the object of a preposition.

> • This is a secret between *you* and *me*.
> • To *whom* do you wish to speak?

Commandment 3 | When a pronoun and noun are side by side, drop the noun.

> • *We* women deserve the award. (We deserve the award.)

C *ommandment 4* | In a comparison, complete the comparison with the verb that would naturally follow.

> • I run faster than *she*. (I run faster than she does.)
> • Is she taller than *I*? (Is she taller than I am?)

C *ommandment 5* | When a pronoun precedes a gerund, make sure it's possessive.

> • *My* cheating has hurt me rather than benefit me.
> • *His* incessant complaining makes me want to smack him.

C *ommandment 6* | When a pronoun follows an indefinite construction, use the nominative case.

> • It was *I* who said that the Yankees suck.
> • Was it *she* who stole the book?

Pronoun Case Exercise 1

➡ *Choose the correct pronoun for each sentence.*

1. We knew it was (he, him).

2. My grandparents took my sister and (I, me) to the concert.

3. That's (he, him) walking the dog on the street.

4. (We, Us) girls are studying how to conquer the men.

5. What were you saying to Paul and (we, us) earlier?

6. It's either you or (he, him) who will win the award.

7. The guests thanked the host and (she, her).

8. Did Jean and (he, him) play violin in the pit?

9. Give (we, us) girls the money as soon as possible.

10. Juanita and (I, me) have matching shoes.

11. Who will tell my dad and (I, me) the truth?

12. I didn't hear the teacher and (they, them) arrive.

13. Juana and (she, her) are active members of the PTA.

14. Of course, I remember you and (she, her).

15. The celebrity granted (she, her) an exclusive interview.

16. The principal gave her friend and (she, her) more detention for being bad.

17. We are glad it wasn't Mina and (she, her) in the accident.

18. It could be (they, them) across the street.

19. The policeman gave Monty and (he, him) a warning.

20. I thought it was (she, her) on the stage.

21. The coach chose Donny and (he, him) to lead the exercises.

22. Luckily, the Bops and (we, us) missed the heavy traffic.

23. Adelaide painted a portrait for (they, them) and (we, us).

24. Is it really (she, her) walking down the road?

25. Would you please stop talking to Carla and (I, me)?

26. The volunteers and (I, me) distributed the posters.

27. Ms. Hodgepodge, the Motleys, and (she, her) went to the picnic.

28. During the busy season, the boss relies on (we, us) workers.

29. I will call Julie and (they, them) tomorrow.

30. (We, Us) science students did our experiment at the fair.

31. (She, Her) and Heathcliff always sit in the last row.

32. Mrs. Lennon said that (we, us) girls inspired her to do great things in life.

33. Mr. Weaver chaperoned the boys and (we, us) during the school trip.

34. The team and (they, them) work well together.

35. Who is running toward (he, him)?

36. Neither the Tigers nor (we, us) Cougars play today?

37. Sunny visited (she, her) and (I, me) in the hospital.

38. I thought it was Babs and (they, them) in the center seats.

39. I haven't heard from Sparky and (she, her) in ages.

40. You and (he, him) have been practicing the roles every day.

 Pronoun Case Exercise 2

 Choose the correct pronoun for each sentence.

1. The three people (who, whom) I like most are me, myself and I.

2. Anybody (who, whom) orders now will receive a free Happy Meal.

3. Neither of the two violinists was the musician (who, whom) the audience cheered.

4. We did not hear (who, whom) the President had named as his head security advisor.

5. The MC said that (whoever, whomever) finishes last can later claim the consolation price.

6. They are curious about (who, whom) you talked to so angrily.

7. The player's reaction was to shout at the referee (who, whom) charged him with the penalty.

8. The science club wants to find a taxodermist (who, whom) will be an exciting guest speaker.

9. Someone called last night, but I don't know (who, whom) she was.

10. Jisun Lee is a woman (who, whom) we should revere.

11. "May I help you?" asked the receptionist. "(Who, Whom) do you wish to see?"

12. When you get to the hotel, give your reservation stub to the person (who, whom) is at the concierge desk.

13. I remember (us, our) exploring the rocky coast of Norway when I was fifteen, and I have wanted to return there ever since.

14. Many people, adults as well as teenagers, waste time worrying about (who, whom) is more popular in their social group.

15. As we waited backstage, I knew in my heart that the pageant was really going to be between Ariel and (I, me).

16. I was so happy to see the new car that I could only gasp to my friend Cole Trickle, "Those wheels were made for you and (I, me)!"

17. Knowing Laurel and Abbot, I thought it had to be (they, them) who had played the joke on me.

18. Polonius said that for the first time the fencing team had elected co-captains, Laertes and (he, him).

19. The President-elect knew exactly (who, whom) he wanted to appoint as Secretary of State.

20. "When you and Heidi were young children," said my grandfather, "I used to enjoy watching you and (she, her) playing with the goats."

Pronoun Case Exercise 3

Choose the correct pronoun for each sentence.

1. Have you lived in Korea as long as (they, them)?

2. Can Mr. Pyo tutor Paul as well as (I, me)?

3. Regina is two feet shorter than (I, me).

4. Can they hit homeruns as often as (we, us)?

5. The medicine will benefit Tony more than (I, me).

6. Is she that much older than (I, me)?

7. I don't know Bonnie as well as (she, her).

8. The exchange student scored higher than (they, them).

9. I understand him better than (she, her).

10. The results show that I do better on spatial problems than (he, him).

Correct any errors in pronoun use.

11. Antonio sat on the bench between Portia and I.

12. When Icarus and I were young, us kids used to love to ride the chariot with his father.

13. The marketplace being closed annoyed us.

14. Both Nausicaa and myself take lute lessons.

15. The two students whom the board nominated were Jennifer and me.

16. The two people in this group whom you can always depend on are Katharine and her.

17. Ulysses, whom I believe is the smartest member of our army, shares the evening newspaper with Nestor and me.

18. Cressida announced to Joe and me that Diomedes and her would do the laundry.

19. When Hera told Athena and Hermes that Zeus was going to retire, all three of us deities felt sad.

20. Their dancing thrilled the audience.

21. If you can't trust Falstaff and her, who can you trust?

22. "We kids are better than the kids on Thebes'team," Oberon said. "So why aren't we doing better than them?"

23. We all looked forward to their singing.

24. They had not been told about us staying overnight.

25. My close friends, Patrocles and he, joined the fight against the Trojans.

26. After him promising to drive us, his car broke down.

27. Someone, either Shylock or he, talked to the Duke of Athens.

28. The coach tried to understand him striking out.

29. The reporters interviewed his uncle and himself.

30. When Ares and I attack together, nobody on the battlefield does better than us.

Chapter 3

PRONOUN REFERENCE

 Pronoun & Antecedent Rules

The function of a pronoun is to replace a noun. This noun is called the antecedent. There are a few simple rules for pronouns and their antecedents.

First, every pronoun must agree with its antecedent in person, number and gender.

> - *Neither* of the girls could find *her* key.
> - *Both* of the *boys* had their keys.
> - *Each* student should remember *his or her* key.

Second, the pronoun reference should be unambiguous. Problems in vague reference arise when the antecedent could be more than one noun, or when the antecedent is not expressed.

Vague	The teacher thought that Joe would be a good choice for president because of his experience with teamwork.
Clear	The teacher thought that Joe would be a good choice for president because of Joe's experience with teamwork.
Vague	Last week I went hunting with our town's finest snipers, but I didn't shoot a single one.
Clear	Last week I went hunting with our town's finest snipers, but I didn't shoot a single target.
Vague	Demonstrations demand determined people, but it isn't always the case.
Clear	Demonstrations demand determined people, but such people are not easy to find.
Vague	Caroline spent years writing music, but none of them ever sold.
Clear	Caroline spent years writing music, but none of her pieces ever sold.
Vague	I ran too fast, which gave me a cramp.
Clear	Having run too fast, I developed a cramp.
Vague	In the newspaper they said that the economy was booming.
Clear	The newspaper article stated that the economy was booming.

Pronoun–Antecedent Agreement Exercise

🔘 *Correct any errors in pronoun-antecedent agreement.*

1. Every one of the speakers at the convention gave their lectures too quickly.

2. If anyone loses their way while exploring the cave, they should use the compass to regain their sense of direction.

3. Each of the snowboarders waxed their boards before leaving the lodge.

4. I believe that anybody has the right to express their opinion.

5. One of the ironic facts of Achieve Academy is that both Joe Park and Mr. Pyo were granted admission into MIT.

6. Neither of the male soloists enunciated their words very clearly.

7. Neither of the newborns were able to recognize its mother's face.

8. All of the students enjoyed their trip to Paris, where they saw the Eiffel Tower.

9. As far as I could see, neither of the women made a mistake while presenting their proposals to the board.

10. No one brought their swimming suits to the party.

Ambiguous Pronoun Reference Exercise

🔘 *Correct any ambiguity in pronoun reference.*

1. Clarence was constantly hallucinating, and that frightened him.

2. Ray was bickering with John, and he looked angry.

3. Pastor Kim came to the house daily, from which a sturdy friendship grew.

4. Raise the telescope to your eye, turning it slowly to the right until it is focused.

5. Our job was to remove the labels from the old artifacts and wash them.

6. President Gore appointed Senator Pat O'Riley as chairman because he was convinced of the importance of the committee's work.

7. One of the passengers told the shuttle bus driver that he had missed the stop.

8. I enjoyed the author's writing style and surrealist plot. It made me want to read her other books.

9. Right after the accountant sent in a report to the treasurer, she became very nervous.

10. A great deal of effort went into planning the rescue mission, hiring the right sort of men, and anticipating every emergency, which accounts for the success of the undertaking.

11. The Chinese were bitter when the United States revoked its MFN status; they said it would harm the economy.

12. The partnership between Joe and Pyo ended when he drew the firm's money from the bank and flew to Korea.

13. Paul is always thinking about EverQuest. It is his only interest.

14. In her vaudeville act Jeanie told jokes, did impersonations, and sang comic songs. This amused her audience.

15. The boys wore roller blades to class which the teacher disapproved of.

16. The air conditioner was leaking badly; it ran all over the living room floor.

17. She is extremely odd, but she hides it from people she doesn't know well.

18. In the epilogue it implies that the hero died a martyr's death.

19. I take many pictures with my camera and consider it an enjoyable hobby.

20. On domestic flights, they don't show any movies.

21. She was a virtuoso cellist, but she never owned a valuable one.

22. Tennis wouldn't cost me so much if I didn't hit so many over the fence.

23. Our guide said the Inuit village was well worth seeing, but it would take three hours.

24. Louis wrote whenever she could find the time, but none of it was ever published.

25. Being neighborly is important because you may need their help someday in an emergency.

26. In some countries, you don't dare express democratic views openly.

27. The people want honest public servants, but that has not always been a virtue of politicians.

28. We spent all day fishing, but we didn't catch a single one.

 Subject–Verb & Pronoun–Antecedent Agreement Exercise

Choose the correct verb or pronoun for each sentence.

1. Jisun is one of those students who always (takes, take) impeccable notes.

2. Diana's greatest problem before a test (is, are) nerves.

3. A team with too many chiefs and not enough Indians (has, have) trouble working as a unit.

4. An adventure novel, The Three Musketeers (has, have) been made into a movie many times.

5. Each of the police cruisers (was, were) communicating with the dispatcher.

6. One of the women pulled (her, their) hamstring in the race.

7. Ms. Lee, in addition to Mr. Park and Ms. Kim, (was, were) asked to make a statement at the PTA meeting.

8. Many a doctor (has, have) a headache on a day when he has to man the emergency room.

9. "(Is, Are) measles contagious?" I asked when I found out my teacher had it.

10. As I shaded my eyes from the bright sun, Doug said, "(Here's, Here are) my new sunglasses. Would you like to borrow them?"

11. Each of the protesters had brought (his, their) signs to the demonstration.

12. The Empire State Building in New York City (is, are) an awesome sight.

13. The number of people seeking jobs in consulting firms (is, are) rising rapidly.

14. Lucy (doesn't, don't) look like her sister Ethel at all.

15. At the dance, some of the food served at the dessert table (was, were) catered.

16. Our school is proud of (its, their) extracurricular activities.

17. My mother thought that fifty-five dollars (was, were) too much to pay for the T-shirt.

18. Janice or the twins (is, are) expecting you to call tonight.

19. Both of your ideas (is, are) insightful.

20. When we got to the airport, we discovered that neither Paul nor John had brought (his, their) passport.

🌑 *Correct any errors in subject-verb or pronoun-antecedent agreement.*

21. One junior, as well as four seniors, have been invited to attend the Milford Youth Council each month.

22. Ten miles are too far for someone to walk unless he is a marathon runner.

23. A gentle snowfall is one of those winter events that is guaranteed to put me into a peaceful mood.

24. During the five hours of deliberation, the jury was often in disagreement.

25. Are the Canary Islands in the Atlantic Ocean?

26. Anyone earning such a low salary will have trouble paying their bills.

27. "Neither of the movies seem to have much hope of making the millions the producers want," commented the film critic.

28. Is there any soda and cookies left from the party?

29. Each of the boys got a stipend for their internship.

30. Every file closet, dresser drawer, and free space were crammed with clothing.

Chapter 4

VERB FORM AND TENSE

Most verbs have three principal forms: present, past and past participle. Errors often occur in the conjugation of the irregular verbs. Familiarize yourself with the following list.

List of Common Irregular Verbs

PRESENT	PAST	PAST PARTICIPLE (add have, has, or had)
arise	arose	arisen
be (am, are)	was, were	been
bear	bore	borne
beat	beaten	beaten
become	became	become
begin	began	begun

bid	bade	bid, bidden
blow	blew	blown
break	broke	broken
bring	brought	brought
build	built	built
buy	bought	bought
catch	caught	caught
choose	chose	chosen
cling	clung	clung
come	came	come
cut	cut	cut
do	did	done
draw	drew	drawn
drink	drank	drunk
drive	drove	driven
eat	ate	eaten
fall	fel	fallen
feed	fed	fed
feel	felt	felt
fight	fought	fought
find	found	found
flee	fled	fled
fling	flung	flung
fly	flew	flown
forget	forgot	forgotten
forgive	forgave	forgiven
freeze	froze	frozen
get	got	gotten

give	gave	given
go	went	gone
grow	grew	grown
hang (a person)	hanged	hanged
hang (an object)	hung	hung
hear	heard	heard
hide	hid	hidden
hold	held	held
hurt	hurt	hurt
keep	kept	kept
know	knew	known
lay	laid	laid
lead	led	led
leave	left	left
lend	lent	lent
lie	lay	lain
light	lit, lighted	lit, lighted
lose	lost	lost
make	made	made
meet	met	met
ride	rode	ridden
ring	rang	rung
rise	rose	risen
run	ran	run
see	saw	seen
send	sent	sent
shake	shook	shaken
shoot	shot	shot

shrink	shrank, shrunk	shrunk, shrunken
sit	sat	sat
slay	slew	slain
sleep	slept	slept
slide	slid	slid
speak	spoke	spoken
spend	spent	spent
spin	spun	spun
spring	sprang, sprung	sprung
stand	stood	stood
steal	stole	stolen
sting	stung	stung
strive	strove	striven
swear	swore	swore
swim	swam	swum
swing	swung	swung
take	took	taken
teach	taught	taught
tear	tore	torn
tell	told	told
think	thought	thought
throw	threw	thrown
wake	waked, woke	waked, woken
wear	wore	worn
weave	wove	woven
win	won	won
wring	wrung	wrung
write	wrote	written

🖊 *Complete each sentence with the correct past or past participle verb form.*

1. The bag was so full that it (burst).

2. The dog was so scared that it (begin) to tremble.

3. You (beat) me at tennis the last time we played.

4. Have you ever (fly) in a Concord jet?

5. James has (break) the school long-jump record.

6. They had (begin) to play when the conductor screamed.

7. Jenny has (go) to the dance with her friends.

8. The dancers (do) their warm-up exercises.

9. Have the players (choose) a captain for the team yet?

10. Toni (draw) pictures on the wall when she was two.

🖊 *Correct any errors in verb form. Some sentences are correct.*

11. She wondered if she had chose the right one.

12. They should have went to Cancun for spring break.

13. Mr. Rogers flew to NeverNeverLand last summer.

14. It was so cold in the basement, the water had froze.

15. One of the children could have fell down the rickety stairs.

16. Some of the doodles were drew with pen and ink.

17. I gave her the rest of my change.

18. They never would have begun if you hadn't helped them.

19. During the cold winter the water pipe had bursted.

20. The adults have drank all the wine.

Complete each sentence with the correct past or past participle verb form.

21. Has the bell (ring) yet?

22. Why have they (tear) up the banners?

23. We had (speak) to the plumber about the leak.

24. I (see) a falling star just now.

25. The rabbit had (spring) out of the bushes.

26. We (see) the parade on television.

27. A few of us had (ride) on the motorcycle.

28. The shortstop (run) toward third base.

29. No one could have (know) what was going to happen.

30. If the phone hadn't (ring), I would still be reading.

Correct any errors in verb form. Some sentences are correct.

31. I have ran too much too quickly – now I have a cramp.

32. Had the children rang the alarm as a prank?

33. Little Tommy has growed two inches taller than I.

34. Ms. Owens seen the garbage men everyday.

35. He has tore his pants on the wire fence.

36. Had she knew they were here, she would have stayed home.

37. You should not have took the best one for yourself.

38. The cowboy swung the lariat and roped the cow.

39. Are you sure he swum fifty lengths of the pool?

40. They're sorry they had not spoke up when they had the chance.

Complete each sentence with the correct past or past participle verb form.

41. The SWAT team (burst) open the door.

42. Waiting in the subzero weather, we almost (freeze).

43. Have the movers (break) anything?

44. They could have (fly) to New York City in two hours.

45. A sudden gust of wind (blow) out the candle.

46. She could not have (fall) more than two flights of stairs.

47. The networks (begin) the new season last Monday.

48. We have (know) them since we were young.

49. They (beat) us only because they cheated.

50. I opened the door, but no one had (ring) the bell.

51. We were (drive) by our commitment to the cause.

52. Will has finally (ride) in a trolley car.

53. During the recent flood, we (drink) bottled water.

54. They (run) five miles yesterday evening.

55. Eng and I (do) much better than we had hoped.

56. Holly has (swim) the 100-meter butterfly race.

57. Shortly after you called, Mom (come) home.

58. The clerk discovered that the cash register had been (steal).

59. We should have (choose) seats closer to the stage.

60. Leann Rimes has (sing) professionally since she was young.

61. The number of applicants to medical schools has (grow) tremendously.

62. We have (speak) to the principal on your behalf.

63. I arrived early, but Sophia had already (go).

64. Do you think he (see) us buying his gift?

65. What in the world (give) them such a crazy idea?

🌑 *Correct any errors in verb form.*

66. As I watched the horror movie, I could feel myself shaking; I knew I had chose the wrong way to relax.

67. Aretha had taken her younger sister to the circus; things went well until the little girl's balloon bursted.

68. When we woke, we saw that the pond was froze.

69. When their parents had went shopping, the twins decided to play some computer games.

70. The criminal was brung before the judge for sentencing.

 ## Basic Tense Sequence of Verbs

Besides telling you what happened in a sentence, verbs tell you when it happened, indicating time. In grammatical terms, this is called tense.

Simple tenses describe actions that happened/happen/will happen at one specific time in the past, present or future.

🐢 Present Tense = now

The *present tense is* used to express something occurring now, at the present time.

> - I <u>am</u> at the house.
> - I <u>go</u> to the house.
> - I <u>am going</u> to the house.
> - I <u>do go</u> to the house.

The *present tense* is also used to indicate a habitual action, or to express a statement that is always true, such as a fact.

🐢 Past Tense = yesterday

The *past tense* is used to express something that occurred in the past but did not continue into the present.

> - I <u>was</u> at the house.
> - I <u>went</u> to the house.
> - I <u>was going</u> to the house.
> - I <u>did go</u> to the house.

🐢 Future Tense = tomorrow

The *future tense* is used to express something that will occur at some time in the future.

> - I <u>will be</u> at the house.
> - I <u>will go</u> to the house.
> - I <u>will be going</u> to the house.

Perfect tenses describe actions in the present, past or future that are still relevant at a later time.

⏳ Present Perfect = action that began at some time in the past and may be continuing now

> - I <u>have been</u> at the house for three hours.
> - I <u>have gone</u> to the house. (and I may still be there)
> - I <u>have been going</u> to the house every day. (on a regular basis)

⏳ Past Perfect = action that has been complete before some other past action

> - I <u>had been</u> at the house two hours before he phoned me.
> - I <u>had gone</u> to the house by the time the storm began.
> - I <u>had been going</u> to the house every day for weeks before they gave me a key.

⏳ Future Perfect = action that will be complete before some other future time or action

> - By noon I <u>will have been</u> at the house for three hours.
> - I <u>will have gone</u> to the house by nine o'clock.
> - I <u>will have been going</u> to the house every day for months by the time we have our company picnic.

Note that the third example sentence of each tense is in *progressive tense* as well. The progressive tense uses the *-ing* form of the verb to indicate that the action being described is in progress.

> - I <u>am going</u> to the house.
> - I <u>was going</u> to the house.
> - I <u>will be going</u> to the house.
> - I <u>have been going</u> to the house every day.
> - I <u>had been going</u> to the house every day for weeks before they gave me a key.
> - I <u>will have been going</u> to the house every day for months by the time we have our company picnic.

The progressive tense is often used in conjunction with another tense to indicate two actions, one of which is in progress while the other is not.

The difference between a gerund (a word that ends in "-ing" but is used as a noun) is that gerunds are not preceded by any form of the "to be" verb, whereas progressive tense verbs must be preceded by a form of the "to be" verb, such as "is," "was," or "was.";

It is not important to memorize the technical names of each tense. However, it is important to understand the purpose of each tense to indicate the correct time relationships between different actions. When describing or interpreting a sequence of actions, consider the choice of tense to fully understand the relationship between different actions in the sentence.

Tense Exercise 1

👉 *Explain the difference in meaning between the sentences in the following pairs.*

* I have met you at 3:00.

* I will have met you at 3:00.

In the first sentence, the action occurred once and ended. In the

----

second sentence, the action will be completed in the future before

----

another action will be completed.

1.

* I took Spanish for three years.

* I have taken Spanish for three years.

2.

* Why had he gone to the doctor?

* Why has he been going to the doctor?

3.

* Has the recipe been followed correctly?

* Had the recipe been followed correctly?

In each of the following items, choose the sentence that matches the meaning given.

4.
> * Maria still likes Patrick.

    a. Maria has liked Patrick for a while.

    b. Maria had liked Patrick for a while.

5.
> * Phillip could be on his way to the bowling alley right now or may be going later.

    a. Phillip is going to the bowling alley.

    b. Phillip will be going to the bowling alley.

6.
> * Pamela is still in jail.

    a. Pamela has been serving her sentence since last year.

    b. Pamela served her sentence last year.

7.
> * Elena was born on Mary and David's wedding day.

    a. Barbara and Steven had had their first child, Elena, when Mary and David got married.

    b. Barbara and Steven had their first child, Elena, when Mary and David got married.

8.
> * Caroline will have finished working two jobs by the time she graduates.

    a. When she graduates from college, Caroline will have worked on a farm and in a department store.

    b. When she graduates from college, Caroline will have been working on a farm and in a department store.

Tense Exercise 2

Correct any tense errors in the sentences below.

1. When I presented my speech before the committee, the members previously studied several reports on educational reform.

2. By then I will receive my high school diploma.

3. Although Derek's skill was demonstrated during the season, he was not selected to play in the post season games.

4. If they had enough money, they could have taken a plane instead of a train.

5. If she forgot the map, we could have been lost.

6. The company hired the exchange student because she lived for many years in Greece.

7. Paul finally appreciated the proverb that a penny saved is a penny earned.

8. If you told me you were going to the mall, I would have gone too.

9. By the time we graduate, Ms. Cargill will be teaching U.S. History for twelve years.

10. When I finally got to the doctor, my wound already stopped bleeding.

11. The judges declared that she performed best during the talent competition.

12. If they would have called sooner, I would have given them a ride.

13. When we reviewed the videotapes of the game, we saw that the other team had been cheating after all.

14. By tomorrow we will be living in New Jersey five years.

15. As I thought about our argument, I was sure you started screaming first.

16. If Gary would have read the advertisement, he could have saved at least 30 dollars on his books.

17. How could I have forgotten that Great Britain included England, Wales, and Scotland?

18. We estimate that when we're in our forties, the level of pollution will have been twice as high as it is today.

19. The employee remembered that the manager has ordered the new equipment last week.

20. Will would have done much better on the test if he was not absent so much.

21. Spending three hours on a review of essay writing, we then worked on irregular verbs.

22. By the time my favorite show was on, I did all my homework.

23. I rewrote the essay that I already typed.

24. We gained two hours when we flew from New Jersey to California because the sun rose in the east.

25. We wanted to have avoided any conflict in our negotiations.

 ## Three Sets of Easily Confused Verbs

There are three sets of verbs that people especially tend to confuse:

S *et 1* | "Lie" vs. "Lay"

Lie means to rest, whereas lay means to put down. If you get confused, try replacing the word with its definition to see which word makes more sense. (More technically speaking, *lie* is an intransitive verb, meaning it does not take an object. Thus the subject takes the action of the verb itself. *Lay*, on the other hand, is transitive, meaning that it can take an object. Thus the subject enacts this verb onto another object.)

Be careful also with their verb forms:

	Lie	Lay
present	I *lie* down.	I *lay* it down.
past	I *lay* down.	I *laid* it down.
past participle	I had *lain* down.	I had *laid* it down.

S *et 2* | "Sit" vs. "Set"

Sit means to be in an upright, sitting position, whereas *set* means to put or to place something. Again, when confused you can replace the word with its definition to check. (Technically, *sit* is intransitive and *set* is transitive, and so these verbs follow the same rules as *lie* and *lay*.)

> - Don't *sit* on the wet paint.
> - *Set* the baby down on the chair.

S *et 3* | "Rise" vs. "Raise"

Rise means to go up, and is intransitive. *Raise* means to make something move upward, and is transitive. Thus the subject itself enacts the verb *rise* whereas the subject enacts the verb *raise* onto another object.

Again, watch out for their verb forms.

	Rise	Raise
present	I *rise* at dawn.	I *raise* the flag.
past	I *rose* at dawn.	I *raised* the flag.
past participle	I had *risen* at dawn.	I had *raised* the flag.

"Lie vs. Lay" Exercise

🔵 *Choose the correct verb for each sentence.*

1. Amy (lay, laid) down for a while.

2. They (lay, laid) their plans before the committee.

3. Don't leave your toys (lying, laying) around the house.

4. If you are not feeling well, you should be (lying, laying) down.

5. I left my books (lying, laying) on the counter.

6. She had just (lain, laid) down when the phone rang.

7. She (lay, laid) her pen down and took a nap.

8. The cat (lay, laid) on a pile of laundry.

9. They (lay, laid) the new asphalt on the pavement.

10. She had (lain, laid) much emphasis on our need to do well.

🔵 *Complete each sentence with the correct verb.*

11. Be careful when you are _____ the new tiles in the bathroom.

12. Why don't you _____ down and take a nap before dinner?

13. The mail is _____ on the table for you to read.

14. After an exhausting day, Tyler Durden _____ on the bed.

15. Tomorrow we will _____ new carpeting in the school.

16. Simone had _____ the keys by the door.

17. The old log had _____ on the beach for years.

18. She _____ on the track while the rushing train approached.

19. Paul _____ the baby down and changed his diapers.

20. The mysterious package _____ on the floor.

Choose the correct verb for each sentence.

1. I never (sit, set) in the balcony at the theater.

2. We (sat, set) up folding chairs for the guests.

3. I may never know who had (sat, set) on my glasses.

4. It makes no difference to me where you (sit, set).

5. After he had struck out for the second time, Joe (sat, set) on the bench.

6. They were (sitting, setting) the cups down on the table.

7. We had (sat, set) our tired bodies on the comfortable sofa.

8. My little sister (sits, sets) quietly while the rest of the kids jump around.

9. Mr. Bob told me to (sit, set) the equipment on the bleachers.

10. Where were the people (sitting, setting) on the bus?

 "Rise vs. Raise" Exercise

Choose the correct verb for each sentence.

1. The rooster (rises, raises) early.

2. Woody Allen and Mia Farrow (rose, raised) many adopted children.

3. The goldfish have been (rising, raising) to the surface to eat their food.

4. This month, the star has been (rising, raising) in the east.

5. Steam was (rising, raising) from the ground.

6. During the Revolutionary War, colonists decided to (rise, raise) up against King George III's rule.

7. The dough has been (rising, raising) for the past hour.

8. Increasing the taxes will (rise, raise) retail prices.

9. The celebrity (rose, raised) from his seat and waved to the crowd.

10. Balloons can (rise, raise) because they contain heated air, which is less dense than the surrounding air.

Confused Verbs Exercise

Choose the correct verb for each sentence.

1. Our dog often (lies, lays) in my lap.

2. We (rose, raised) our hands to speak in class.

3. The man should (lie, lay) on his side to stop snoring.

4. We spent the evening (lying, laying) in front of the fire.

5. Last night's victory really (rose, raised) the team's morale.

6. Tempers (rose, raised) as the debate progressed.

7. You must (lie, lay) on a padded surface to do exercises.

8. Haven't they (sat, set) down the piano yet?

9. The robbers are (lying, laying) in wait for their prey.

10. Would you please (sit, set) with us?

 **Subjunctive Mood**

The subjunctive mood is used to express a condition contrary to fact or to express a wish. With the subjunctive mood, you must conjugate the verb differently.

Present indicative		Present subjunctive	
singular	*plural*	*singular*	*plural*
I am	we are	(if) I be	(if) we be
you are	you are	(if) you be	(if) you be
s/he is	they are	(if) s/he be	(if) they be

ex) We recommended that she *be* invited to speak.

They urged that Thad *be* reinstated.

We move that Alma *be* nominated.

Past indicative		Past subjunctive	
singular	*plural*	*singular*	*plural*
I was	we were	(if) I were	(if) we were
you were	you were	(if) you were	(if) you were
s/he was	they were	(if) s/he were	(if) they were

"contrary to fact" ex) If I *were* [not *was*] you, I would be very confident.

[I am not you.]

If Tom *were* [not *was*] dumber, he'd be a rock.

[He is not dumber.]

Diane teased me as though she *were* [not *was*] my friend. [She is not my friend.]

"wish" *ex)* I wish I *were* [not *was*] a movie star.

I wish Clara *were* [not *was*] my friend.

✎ Identifying Subjunctive Mood Exercise

🔵 *Identify the mood of the verb underlined in each sentence below by using the following code:*

S (subjunctive)   **I** (indicative)

Example   *If the party* <u>were</u> *held earlier during the day, we could use the auditorium for practice at night.*

1. The gap between your mouth and nose <u>is</u> known as the hiatus.

2. I insists that the muffins <u>be</u> made with blueberries.

3. The show would be better if the cast <u>were</u> more familiar with their lines.

4. If I <u>were</u> a man, I'd be much less intelligent than I am now.

5. Demands that women <u>become</u> enfranchised were granted in 1920.

6. Since I <u>was</u> going to the mall, Candy decided that she would go also.

7. I ask that you <u>put</u> out that cigar.

8. Joe felt as if he <u>were</u> not treated kindly.

9. The preacher <u>urged</u> the congregation not to fall into sin.

10. I would be very tan if I <u>were</u> to live in the South.

Some of the following sentences contain errors in the use of the subjunctive mood. Revise accordingly.

1. I wish I was able to go to the game, but I have to study.

2. "I wish it was next year already so that I would be in college," she said.

3. We often complain about working too many hours, but if we were to work fewer, we would be complaining about smaller paychecks.

4. "I wish this movie was shorter," I sighed as we entered the fourth hour of screening.

5. Eric lost many of his friends because he acted as if he were better than they.

6. If wrestling was less violent, perhaps many people would respect it more.

7. Rolling another gutter ball, Chris moaned, "I wish I was a better bowler!"

8. I was happy all day because it seemed as though it was Friday, but then I realized that it was actually Thursday.

9. Carrie insisted that every member of the union be given a raise.

10. I'd be a lobster fisherman if I was a native of Maine.

Choose the correct form of the verb for each sentence below.

1. We demand that a new teacher (be, is) hired.

2. The teacher insisted that we (stop, stops) coming to class in our roller blades.

3. The principal insists that Hank (come, comes) to her office at once.

4. Even though the prom isn't until spring, Taylor acts as if she (was, were) already picked prom queen.

5. If I (was, were) you, I would want to die.

6. Heaven (forbid, forbids) that the sky fall down.

7. Mr. Pyo demands that Jong Woo (prepare, prepares) diligently for each test.

8. I think James (was, were) asleep when the bed collapsed.

9. (Come, Comes) what may, I shall forever believe in his innocence.

10. I wish I (own, owned) a motorcycle.

11. I wish the wallpaper (was, were) lighter since the room is so small.

12. I request that the Board of Elections (pay, pays) particular attention to votes cast in the Twelfth District, where all the town cemeteries are located.

13. I wish she (was, were) taking the SAT II Writing test in my place.

14. I move that nominations (be, are) re-opened.

Choose the correct verb for each sentence.

1. During the winter, many of the town's water mains (burst, bursted) as they froze in the cold.

2. Whenever Joe sits down to watch television, his kitty Derek (lies, lays) down in his lap.

3. If I (was, were) Queen of England, I would invade and conquer France.

4. Olympic swimmer Cristina Teuscher (swam, swum) her part of the medley in record time.

5. If I (had, would have) told the truth in the first place, the situation would have been much easier to handle.

6. (Cooking, Having cooked) a delicious Thanksgiving meal, the soup kitchen workers were given much praise and gratitude from their homeless guests.

7. When the math team came in second, the members were upset because they (hoped, had hoped) to take first place.

8. Because we did not add the proper amount of yeast, the loaves of bread failed to (raise, rise).

9. Terry died because he (was hit, had been hit) by lightning.

10. The five gymnasts are pleased (to qualify, to have qualified) for the Olympic team.

11. After I had (wrote, written) my essay for my college application, I heaved a sigh of relief.

12. I wished that there (was, were) a good movie playing tonight.

13. Because he had starred in various commercials, Davey hoped (to pursue, to have pursued) an acting career.

14. (Lie, Lay) your work aside and relax for a few minutes.

15. In 2000, Marian Jones, who had promised to win five gold medals, was ecstatic when she became the first to have (won, had won) give gold medals at one Olympics.

Verb Usage Review Exercise

Some of the following sentences contain errors in verb usage. Revise accordingly.

1. If we had the chance, we would have stopped by your house.

2. For the vacation they planned to have gone skiing.

3. When we saw the group perform, Mariah, the lead vocalist, just broke her contract with a big recording company.

4. If you would have done your homework yesterday, you could have gone to the concert with us.

5. When I enter college, my parents will be married thirty years.

6. If I was more confident, I could try out for the musical.

7. The bank has counted the money and has lain it in the vault.

8. Why don't you ask if they already seen that movie?

9. I never realized that hurricanes and typhoons were really the same thing.

10. As soon as we returned to the gym, we discovered that someone took our books and bags.

11. If I had begun my chores this morning, I would have finished in time to go to the show.

12. We swum to shore when we spotted the shark.

13. Her report explained that shock waves from earthquakes were recorded on seismographs.

14. As the climbers ascended the mountain, they noticed a shiny object laying on the ledge beneath them.

15. If we would have had the engine tuned, I'm sure we would not be stranded on the highway now.

16. If they weren't too proud to ask, I'd have been glad to help them do the assignment.

17. As the journalist interviewed the senatorial candidate, she realized that the batteries went dead in the tape recorder.

18. They had forgotten that yesterday was my birthday.

19. The shoppers laid down their purchases carefully.

20. James, our new supervisor, worked for this company for the past 20 years.

 ## Active and Passive Voice

A verb is in the *active voice* when it expresses an action performed *by* its subject. A verb is in the *passive voice* when it expresses an action performed *upon* its subject or when the subject is the result of the action.

active voice	The boy threw the ball. (subject acting)
passive voice	The ball was thrown by a boy. (subject acted upon)

Note that though the sentences indicate identical actions, the emphasis is differs. In the active voice sentence, the emphasis is on *car*, whereas in the passive voice sentence, the emphasis is on *tree*.

The choice between the active and passive voices is usually a matter of taste, not of correctness. However, it is important to remember that a passive verb is usually less forceful than an active one and that a long succession of passive verbs usually produces an awkward effect.

weak passive	The performance was completed with a triple axle as done by Nikki.
active	Nikki completed the performance when she a triple axle.
weak passive	Steady showers were hoped for by us, but a hurricane was not wanted by us.
active	We hoped for steady showers, but we didn't want a hurricane.
succession of passives	I was asked by Ms. Choi to visit her orphanage for unwanted children. Rows of beds had been placed along both sides of a room. First a baby boy was shown to me. Elsewhere, a crying girl was being comforted by an assistant. Ms. Choi said that so many unwanted chidren had been brought to her, it was difficult for all of them to be housed there. It was agreed by us that the responsibility of having a child should be understood by people before a child is conceived.

Thus use the passive voice sparingly. There are, however, some cases in which the passive voice should be used.

(1) Use the passive voice to express an action in which the actor is unknown.

> *ex)* All the seats had been filled up in five minutes.

(2) Use the passive voice to express an action in which it is desirable not to disclose the actor.

> *ex)* Poor judgment was used in making this decision.

(3) Use the passive voice to express an action in which you use to emphasize the object of the action.

> *ex)* Spaghetti was invented by the Chinese.
> The heroes were cheered by the swarming crowds.
> Britney Spears has been emulated by many young, hopeful singers.

Chapter 5

ADJ, ADV & COMPARISONS

An adjective is a modifier that describes a noun. An adverb is a modifier that describes a verb, an adjective, or another adverb. A good rule of thumb to use when distinguishing between the two is to look at the ending of the word. For instance, most adverbs end in ~*ly*. However, not all adverbs end in ~*ly* and a few adjectives end in ~*ly*. Also, some words have the same form whether used as an adjective or adverb.

adjectives	adverbs	adjectives ending in ~ly
a *short* race	She stopped *short*.	*nightly* walk.
a *close* call	Stand *close* to me.	*bodily* harm
a *high* shelf.	She jumped *high*.	*hourly* pay
a *right* answer	Do it *right*.	*unfriendly* man
a *first* time	She left *first*.	*lively* beat
a *hard* problem	He tried *hard*.	*seemly* choice
a *straight* path	Drive *straight*.	*early* class
a *last* chance	We play *last*.	*likely* area
a *fast* start	Walk *fast*.	*weekly* meeting

S et 1 | "Bad" vs. "Badly"

Two commonly confused adjective and adverb are *bad* and *badly*. Remember that linking verbs are usually followed by adjectives.

linking verbs:

appear	grow	seem	stay
become	look	smell	taste
feel	remain	sound	

Thus, you feel bad, not badly.

> • Joan feels *bad* about the broken vase.
> • The warped record sounds *bad.*

> • I performed *badly* in the contest.
> • I need to take a shower *badly.*

S et 2 | "Well" vs. "Good"

Well may be used as either an adjective or an adverb. As an adjective, *well* has three meanings:

(1) to be in good health:

> • He feels *well.*   • He seems *well.*

(2) to appear well-dressed or well-groomed:

> • She looks *well* in that dress.

(3) to be satisfactory:

> • All is *well.*

Good is always an adjective, and should never be used to modify a verb.

 Adj/Adv Exercise

🔴 *Revise any errors in modifiers in the sentences below.*

1. Parmesan cheese smells very bad.

2. These new clothes my aunt bought for me do not fit me good at all.

3. Some shades of purple and blue go well together.

4. Samantha feels bad about forgetting your birthday.

5. "I'm sure I did good on that test," Paul confidently remarked.

6. "Life can't be treating you all that bad," I told my sister.

7. The players did good towards the end of the game.

8. I am glad to see you looking well after the operation.

9. After she had failed the exam, Karen felt very bad.

10. Let's hope the rest of the day doesn't go this bad.

11. Mr. Pyo is a good teacher who prepares his lessons well.

12. Learning to dance good takes practice.

13. After a lot of exercise, a cold glass of water tastes good.

14. This old watch has been running fairly good.

15. We didn't win, but we played well.

16. If the milk smells badly, don't drink it.

17. The whole day has gone bad for me.

18. I didn't do as well on the test as I thought I had.

19. Fortunately, no one was hurt bad in the accident.

20. Rehearsals are going as well as can be expected.

21. I tried to sing as good as she sang.

22. I slept extremely well last night.

23. Monica seems good enough to leave the hospital.

24. I could not see the game very good from my seat.

25. My sneakers do not look well anymore.

 ## Comparison of Adjectives & Adverbs

Comparison refers to the change in the form of adjectives and adverbs when they indicate the degree of the qualities they express. There are three degrees of comparison: *positive, comparative,* and *superlative.*

Most adjectives and adverbs of one syllable form their comparative and superlative degrees by adding ~*er* and ~*est.*

positive	comparative	superlative
tall	taller	tallest
hot	hotter	hottest
quick	quicker	quickest

Some adjectives of two syllables form their degrees by adding the suffixes or by using *more* and *most*.

pretty	prettier	prettiest
agile	more agile	most agile

Adjectives of more than two syllables and adverbs ending in *~ly* usually form their degrees by using *more* and *most*.

delightful	more delightful	most delightful
quietly	more quietly	most quietly

Comparison to show lesser degrees is done by using *less* and *least* before the adjective or adverb.

weak	less weak	least weak
contented	less contented	least contented
urgently	less urgently	least urgently

Some adjectives and adverbs do not follow the regular methods of forming their degrees, and so are irregular.

bad	worse	worst
good well	better	best
many much	more	most

Rules for Comparisons

Rule 1 | Use the comparative degree when comparing two things; use the superlative degree when comparing more than two.

Bad	Although Jill and Jane are twins, Jill is *tallest*.
Good	Although Jill and Jane are twins, Jill is *taller*.

Rule 2 | Include the word other or else when comparing one thing with a group of which it is a part.

Bad	Diamond, a crystalline form of carbon, is harder than any mineral in the world. (Diamond is harder than all other minerals, including itself. Impossible!)
Good	Diamond, a crystalline form of carbon, is harder than any *other* mineral in the world.

Bad	I am a better teacher than anyone in this academy. (This implies that I am not a teacher at the academy.)
Good	I am a better teacher than anyone *else* in this academy.

Rule 3 | Avoid double comparisons.

Bad	Joe is a *more faster* swimmer than I.
Good	Joe is a *faster* swimmer than I.

R *ule 4* | Make sure the comparison is complete. Incomplete comparisons cause ambiguity.

> • Pansy visited her aunt longer than Posey.

This sentence can mean either that Pansy spent a longer time with her aunt than Posey, or that Pansy spent more time with her aunt than she did with Posey. To clarify, complete the comparison.

> *or*
> • Pansy visited her aunt longer than Posey did.
> • Pansy visited her aunt longer than she visited Posey.

R *ule 5* | When comparing with the word "as," make sure that you complete the comparison with the second "as."

> • I am as hungry *as* you are.
> • I think I will do *as* well *as* if not better than you.

R *ule 6* | Make sure the comparison is parallel.

> • Skiing is not as fun as going snowboarding.
>   (This is not parallel.)
> • Skiing is not as fun as snowboarding.
>   (This is parallel.)

R *ule 7* | Make sure that the comparison is logical. A comparison is logical only when it is between like objects.

> • Your hair is dirtier than everyone else in this class.
>   (Illogical comparison of *hair* and *people*.)
> • Your hair is dirtier than everyone else's hair in this class.   (Logical)
> • Your hair is dirtier than everyone else's in this class.   (Logical)
> • Your hair is dirtier than that of everyone else in this class.   (Logical)

R*ule 8* | Remember that not all adjectives and adverbs can be used in comparisons.

> • I want a more equal share of the profits. (But how can something be more equal? It's equal or it's not - there is no in between.)

Some adjectives and adverbs that do not have degrees:

> perfect/ly   unique/ly   equal/ly   superior/inferior

R*ule 9* | Do not begin your sentences with adverbs.

> • Hopefully it will rain today. (This means that the rain will fall in a hopeful way, which is not what you mean.)
>   → I hope that it will rain today.
> • Thankfully the speaker was on time. (This means the speaker was thankful, when you mean that you were thankful.)
>   → I am thankful that the speaker was on time.

⬤ *Some of the following sentences contain errors in the use of comparative and superlative degrees of adjectives. Revise accordingly.*

1. Sue made the mistake of buying a darker shade of paint than she needed for the small room.

2. Miles is taking more classes than I.

3. My parents read both a morning and an evening newspaper, but I think the morning paper is best.

4. We thought Patti was the most talented of all the actors in the community play.

5. People need to develop a more clear sense of self-reliance.

6. Jennifer thought nothing could be as bad as the snow; however, when the ice storm arrived, she said, "This weather is even worser!"

7. He thought she seemed gracefuller than the other model.

8. Both twins, Michaela and Carmela, have brown eyes, but Michaela's are darkest.

9. Dividing the pie in two, Patty took the least and gave me the larger portion.

10. The picture on this set is much more clearer than on that one.

 Illogical Comparison Exercise

⬤ *Determine if the comparisons in the sentences below are logical. Correct any illogical comparisons.*

1. Joe is the worse batter in his whole team.

2. Who's prettiest, Jeanie or Janie?

3. This is as good as it gets.

4. It was the most perfect experience I have ever had.

5. This horse is as fast or even faster than the other horse.

6. I demand a more equal share of the profits.

7. She is a better musician than any of the others in her section.

8. Howard is faster than any sprinter in his class.

9. She is definitely as capable or more capable than her brother.

10. The technology of Japan is comparable to that of Korea.

11. I am only allowed to choose between these two items to qualify for the discount.

12. He not only enjoys playing Beethoven but also listening to that master's symphonies.

13. Los Angeles' roads are much better paved than Boston's.

14. Janet is as good an equestrian as anyone else on her team.

15. I am more superior to you at this sport.

16. I don't ever remember having studied algebra.

17. The flowers in my garden are just as pretty as the ones in the city's gardens.

18. Although I found the museum in Paris fascinating, I liked it less than Rome.

19. Phil works faster than Dan on most jobs.

20. The aesthetic development of the Romans is comparable to the Greeks.

Chapter 6

PARALLEL STRUCTURE

 Rules on Parallel Structure

Parallel ideas should be expressed in parallel grammatical forms. That is, if different elements of the sentence carry equal weight, they should all be expressed in the same way. If there is a lack of parallel structure, the sentence sounds awkward. For this reason, nouns are placed with nouns, adjectives with adjectives, phrases with phrases, and clauses with clauses. Likewise, when articles are left out or pronouns omitted, the meaning of the sentence becomes ambiguous.

Bad	Katie said that her favorite games were checkers, handball, and playing Frisbee. (noun, noun, gerund phrase)
Good	Katie said that her favorite games were checkers, handball, and Frisbee. (noun, noun, noun)

Bad	Critics wrote that the play was boring, the acting was poor, and it was too long. (adjective, clause, clause)
Good	Critics wrote that the movie was boring, poorly acted, and too long. (three predicate adjectives after *was*)
Bad	Drew likes swimming, bike trips, and camping. (gerund, noun phrase, gerund)
Good	Drew likes swimming, bicycling, and camping. (gerund, gerund, gerund)
Bad	Dad knows what Amy wants, plans for her party, and needs at the grocery store.
Good	Dad knows what Amy wants, what she has planned for her party, and what she needs at the grocery store.
Bad	Ben is not only head of the department, but also the staff of instructors. (*not only* is misplaced)
Good	Ben is head not only of the department, but also of the instructors' staff. (note the repeated *of*)
Bad	I saw that Jane both appreciated the swimming and the diving. (*both* is misplaced)
Good	I saw that Jane appreciated both the swimming and the diving.
Bad	Jenny wanted the car more for its looks than for how it would help her get to work. (noun contrasted with clause)
Good	Jenny wanted the car more for its looks than for its practicality. (paired preposition-noun phrases)

Parallel Structure Exercise 1

Correct all errors.

1. Before the wedding I talked with the caterer and MC.

2. Cruella DeVille has smooth, leathery skin; long, thin finger nails; and she has a body that is thin.

3. Reading non-fiction no longer interests me as much as fiction.

4. Spider eggs are laid in a sac, carried on the female body, and then they deposit them in hidden crevices.

5. The police tried both persuasion and to force their way into the compound.

6. A typical grasshopper lives as a nymph for about a year, and as an adult its life lasts about one and a half years.

7. Mrs. Selwyn is not only a friend of Evelina but also of Mr. Villars.

8. We might not only view SAT academies with revulsion but also interest.

9. We decided to attack all aspects of the problem - social, political, and cost.

10. The wet track was a greater handicap to the home team than their opposition.

11. Ms. Connor's lectures are easier to comprehend than Ms. Moore.

12. Its simple structure, expendability, and because you can find one anywhere, make the common field mouse easy to study.

13. According to my teacher, Hamlet showed exceptional self-awareness but that he dawdled in his actions.

14. Flushable toilets are not only found in urban areas but also in the tropics.

15. M & Ms may be dark brown, pale brown, or of a green color that looks minty.

16. Her piece was praised more for its style than for what it communicated.

17. The new secretary soon proved herself to be not only unfriendly but also dishonest.

18. Piranhas will eat anything, but they especially like tough meat and foods that are starchy.

19. Mr. Coverley both felt the satisfaction of victory and the disappointment of defeat.

20. The cockroach both is the most primitive living winged insect and the most ancient fossil insect.

21. We have as much to learn from the cockroach's evolution as there is to gain from extinguishing it.

22. Lydia always chose activities that were more interesting than the other students.

23. We feel certain that she is capable, she will succeed, and you will be proud of her.

24. A modern director's interpretation of Hamlet is very different from a nineteenth-century director.

25. She not only was industrious, but she could be depended on.

26. The speech of cultivated Britons is not so different as it used to be from Americans.

🖊 *Correct the faulty parallel structure in the following sentences.*

1. I detest teachers who ignore the well-behaved children and the delinquents are given their full attention.

2. The fear of the number 13 is called triskaidekaphobia; panaphobia is the name for the fear of everything.

3. These three prevent most accidents: courtesy, common sense, and to be cautious.

4. He is such a loud person that ear plugs are worn by his family members.

🖊 *Correct the following sentences for parallel structure.*

5. The cat flicked its tail, meowed, and stalks away.

6. Sunny has big muscles and is very strong.

7. We told the teacher that Andy would erase the board, the sweeping would be done by Regina, and the garbage would be taken out by Carley.

8. He likes to run, go skiing, and jogging.

9. I washed the car, I dried off the car, and as for waxing it, I did that, too.

10. Johnny did the yard work, Janie did the laundry, but nothing was done by Josh.

11. If one gives enough effort, you can conquer any obstacle.

12. He likes running and to go skiing and jogging.

13. Compare the painting in the book with the museum.

14. The speaker was oblivious and undisturbed by the rude noises made by the kids.

15. He gave Christmas presents both to his hostess and her sister.

16. This subpoena is either for you or your brother.

17. Joe Kang is short but has strength.

Chapter 7

MISPLACED & DANGLING MODIFIERS

 Rules on Misplaced & Dangling Modifiers

A modifier is anything that describes something else. As you should know already, an adjective is a modifier of a noun, and an adverb is a modifier of a verb or another adverb. An entire phrase or clause can also act as a modifier. Ideally, a modifier should stay as close as possible to whatever it is describing. The farther away it gets, the more confusion arises. Modifiers that dangle at the beginning of a sentence or that occur in odd places create a grammatical mess.

Bad	Babs called her mom from Maine. (Is Babs in Oregon or is her mom from Maine?)
Good	When Babs was in Maine, she called her mom. Babs called her mom who lives in Maine.

Bad	Blowing across the dunes, the dog sniffed the salty air. (The dog was blowing across the dunes?)
Good	The dog sniffed the salty air blowing across the dunes.

Bad	Looking at the cathedral, the past seems alive. (The past is looking at the cathedral?)
Good	When I look at the cathedral, the past seems alive.

Bad	The dean gives a talk on minding our manners in school about every two weeks. (The dean wants you to behave only every two weeks?)
Good	About every two weeks, the dean gives a talk on minding our manners in school.

Watch out also for the one word modifiers, such as *only*.

Bad	I only remember two problems from the test. (In your entire memory bank there exist only two items?)
Good	I remember only two problems from the test. (Out of all the problems on the test, you remember two of them.)

Misplaced Modifiers Exercise

Correct any misplaced modifiers.

1. The Navy Seal commander was honored for his valor, but he was haunted by the memory of the men who had died unrecognized in the black ops.

2. The castle moat has a drawbridge to permit the passage of people and cargo that no one but the drawbridge-raiser can manipulate.

3. Indiana Jones described his archeological finds he made in the jungle in our anthropology class.

4. Many meetings have been held to make arrangements for Elian Gonzalez' return in Miami, Florida.

5. The company now runs a daycare center for any employee who has children full-time.

6. Our recon scout sighted a figure through binoculars that she could not identify.

7. I bought a high-tech microwave for the office kitchen, which gave everyone a great deal of pleasure.

8. The dormitory was funded by Miss Rogers, who later became Mrs. Datsun, at a cost of 2 million.

9. The President discussed the possibility of filling every pothole in the United States with members of the Congress.

10. Father bought a new radio from a fast-talking salesclerk that was supposed to make soothing sounds at night to promote sleep.

Correct any dangling modifiers.

1. Left alone in the house, the thunderstorm terrified him.

2. Representing the defendant, the lawyer's evidence was strong.

3. To win the tournament this year, our practice sessions were lengthened.

4. Running up the wet stairs, her foot slipped on the step.

5. To keep food fresh, aluminum foil is more effective than saran wrap.

6. When crossing the street, any cars should be avoided.

7. While joking mockingly with friends, tempers began to flare.

8. After flying in mist for two hours, the thick clouds began to disperse, and the pilot was able to see better.

9. Enormous and visually striking, the bystanders all stopped to marvel at the statue.

10. After working in the office all day, little strength was left for the evening outing.

 Dangling & Misplaced Modifiers Exercise

Correct any dangling or misplaced modifiers.

1. Before gaining admittance to his apartment, a bell must be rung.

2. Stumbling blindly in the fog, I saw a man appear.

3. Having run for many weeks, critics considered the performance a success.

4. To successfully market a product, its design must be user-friendly as well as aesthetically pleasing.

5. After having helped the old man cross the street, the rest of the walk was uneventful.

6. To win the approval of the judge, all aspects of the motion must be argued carefully.

7. To win over a hostile audience, the jokes have to be twice as good.

8. Standing in the hallway, the lockers are on constant watch by the monitor.

9. To reach my office by 8:15, the train must be on time.

10. Did you hear the news about the explosion on the ship on the radio?

11. Stuck in traffic for hours, a feeling of frustration is no surprise.

12. He went to the old church to pray for the people on Cemetery Hill.

13. Having used all natural ingredients, a healthy dinner is certain.

14. In his entire family, his wife only loved him.

15. Upon picking up the phone, the volume was lowered.

 More Dangling & Misplaced Modifiers Exercise

● *Correct any dangling or misplaced modifiers.*

1. One can see the breadth of an entire state, flying at an altitude of several thousand feet.

2. Living constantly under the eyes of a prison guard, his anxiety increased until he became insane.

3. The principal gave a detention notice to one of the students with his signature.

4. Plans for a new gymnasium have finally been approved after four years of bickering to replace the abandoned football field.5. We saw a pack of wild wolves on the way to our Grandmother's house.

6. To succeed in anything, a great deal of persistence is key.

7. Cameron wanted to know before the contest began what the referee had said to the two captains.

8. This bank approves loans to individuals with good credit history of any size.

9. While trying to prepare dinner, the smoke alarm went off.

10. A tropical insect was shown to me by the museum's curator that had curious markings I have never seen before.

Chapter 8

SENTENCES

 Sentence Revision Exercise

🖋 *Correct any errors in parallelism, misplaced modifiers and dangling modifiers. Some sentences have more than one error.*

1. Walking takes longer, but it is better for your joints than to run.

2. I was having a great time at the party and no anxieties about my future plans.

3. To get into the exclusive club we tried both persuasion and bribing the bouncer.

4. You can arrive in time to catch the plane, if you are leaving at ten o'clock.

5. To go to toy stores and going roller-skating were childhood treats.

6. If hit accidentally by a ball, no protest should be registered.

7. Jose had been appointed not only president of the company but the softball team, too.

8. He saw Lester working out through the window.

9. Gill didn't know whether to put the dishwashing liquid in before the water or should he do it in the reverse order.

10. She sometimes goes to school poorly groomed, wearing dirty jeans, and without brushing her hair.

 Punctuation & Sentences

Punctuation becomes relevant to our study in regard to sentence fragments, run-on sentences and comma splices.

Sentence fragments are statements that express incomplete thoughts and often start with subordinating conjunctions or participles.

> • Because I was sick last Monday.
> • While the audience cheered and hollered from their seats.
> • Having no place to go but the shelter.
> • Feeling alone and depressed on a rainy day.

Run-on sentences express complete thoughts, but join two independent clauses as one. Often the two clauses are separated by a comma, making the run-on sentence a *comma splice*.

> • There was no water in the refrigerator, I drank orange juice instead.

An often misused piece of punctuation is the *semi-colon*. The correct use of the semi-colon is exactly like that of a period. The semi-colon does not act as a comma, and should have independent clauses on either side. The only difference between a semi-colon and a period is stylistic. The semi-colon gives more of a pause between independent clauses, whereas the period gives a full stop. Thus when you want to express two very closely related ideas, it's a good idea to use a semi-colon.

> • I adore Nature Valley granola bars; I eat them every morning.
> • The book had been left out in the rain; it was ruined.
>
> *vs.*
>
> • I drink my coffee black. Joe likes his with milk and sugar.

 Conjunctions

Conjunctions connect words, phrases, or clauses.

- **Coordinate conjunctions**: *connects words, phrases or clauses of equal structural rank*

and	but	or	nor	for

- **Subordinate conjunctions**: *connects a dependent clause with an independent clause*

after	if	when
although	since	where
as	that	wherever
as if	though	which
because	unless	while
before	until	who
except	what	why

Correlative conjunctions: *paired conjunctions that connect words or phrases of equal structural value.*

as much...as	not...but
both...and	not merely...but
either...or	not only...but
first...second	not only...but also
less...than	not so much...as
more...than	now...then
neither...nor	whether...or

Conjunctive adverbs: *separate two independent clauses with a semicolon or period*

consequently	moreover
furthermore	nevertheless
for example	on the other hand
for instance	otherwise
hence	therefore
however	thus
instead	so

Run-on Sentences Exercise

🔵 *Correct all run-on sentences.*

1. First try to do these grammar problems by yourself, if you can't do it, don't look at your friend's book, ask the teacher for help.

2. We have a pet cat, it always scratches the furniture and sheds hair all over the place.

3. A suggestion box has been placed in the hall just outside the supervisor's office, employees can, by this means, express their complaints about the company, they should not sign their names.

4. A new committee is being formed for the study of social delinquency, instead of just identifying problems, psychiatrists will create solutions.

5. Eddie took an art elective and discovered he had talent, now he spends his afternoons at the art academy improving his technique.

6. At an advanced age Jamaica Kinkaid began to write the story of her unique life, at least she thought her life had been unique.

7. The astounding technological developments of one decade are taken for granted in the next, mp3s and the DVDs, for instance, are nothing new today.

8. Jacques Cousteau, the marine explorer, discovered rare fish on his expeditions to Mexico and South America, these discoveries were of great interest to science.

9. Kittens are comical creatures, they are always busy chasing their tails.

10. In history this year we are studying about ways to solve the division in our political system, so far we have covered strategies of reconciliation and bipartisanship.

Correct any errors.

1. I have never known anyone who has a better work ethic than Gary; who always finished his work long before deadline, he usually had it done perfectly as well.

2. I asked Gary to help me on a project once. When I was particularly desperate, I hadn't been getting good reviews from my supervisor for several weeks.

3. Mr. Campanella urges all of the orchestra members to continue to study their instruments in high school. Because he knows that as they get older, many students stop taking music lessons, academics and other extracurricular activities take up most of their time.

4. A bulldozer was brought to move the huge mound of dirt onto the new foundation. Several tons of dirt were transported in one easy move; almost as though they were feathers.

5. Everyone was asking questions about the new kid, Daniel La Russo. Where he was from and what he was wearing, wild rumors had been circulating.

6. The village's water supply has been threatened. An old oil barrel having leaked into the single well during the past few days.

7. I learned to like fantasy novels when I read Anne McCaffrey, her writing appealed to me. Because of its strong narrative style and use of imagination.

8. I have learned to recognize several kinds of people. Especially the kind that gets pleasure out of being mean, when I see one of these coming, I run for cover.

9. Women's colleges were established in America in the nineteenth century. During the Victorian period, when girls were considered frail flowers to be kept safe and separate.

10. Audiences appeared to enjoy the play, however, the reviews in the papers were unfavorable.

Chapter 9

DICTION & WORD USAGE

 **Idioms**

An idiom is a phrase that is put together by convention, not by any specific rules.

For example, you would say,

> This is *different from* that.

but not,

> This is *different by* that.

Different verbs pair with different prepositions. Some verbs pair with more than one preposition, depending on the object of the preposition. With idioms you either know it or you don't, so familiarize yourself with the following list.

List of Common Idioms

abide by/in Everyone should *abide by* the law.

abound in/with This pond abounds *in/with* fish.

accompanied by (a person) The salesman was *accompanied by* the buyer.

accompanied with (an object) He accompanied the closing of the *contract with* a gift.

accuse of You cannot *accuse* me *of* something I did not do.

acquiesce in The executives were compelled to *acquiesce in* the director's policy.

acquit of The manager was *acquitted of* the charges against him.

adept in/at He is *adept in/at* typing.

agree to (an offer) The firm *agrees to* your payment in settlement of the claim.

agree upon/on (a plan) We must agree *upon/on* the best method.

agree with (a person) I *agree with* the doctor.

angry about (an event) I am very *angry about* the high unemployment rate.

angry at (a thing) The child is *angry at* his stuffed animals.

angry with (a person) We were *angry with* the careless attendant. (Mad means insane.)

apologize for I *apologize for* my dog's bad behavior.

appropriate for The gown is also *appropriate for* a dinner dance.

approve of I cannot *approve of* such inhumane acts.

argue about (an issue) We *argued* all night *about* the state of the nation's economy.

argue with (a person) I *argue with* Joe everyday about something.

arrive at We *arrived at* our destination ahead of schedule.

available for (a purpose) The specialist is *available for* a consultation now.

available to (a person) What course of action is *available to* you at this time?

averse to The President is *averse to* increasing his staff.

blame for How can you *blame* me *for* that?

capable of Psychopaths are *capable of* horrendous acts of violence.

center on The debate will *center on* education.

cognizant of He was not *cognizant of* dissension among the workers.

coincide with Your wishes *coincide with* mine in this situation.

commensurate with What you earn will be *commensurate with* the amount of effort you apply to your task.

compatible with In a successful marriage the husband's values are *compatible with* those of his wife.

comply with If you do not *comply with* the law, you will be arrested.

conducive to The employer's kindness is *conducive to* good work.

conform to/with The average person *conforms to/with* the opinion of the majority.

consist of Bologna meat *consists of* many meat by-products.

conversant with We need a salesman who is fully *conversant with* what he is selling.

desirous of We are not *desirous of* a price increase.

detract from This one poorly constructed sentence *detracts from* the quality of your entire essay.

different from This new machine is *different from* the old one.

differ from (a thing in appearance) A coat *differs from* a cape in that the former has sleeves.

differ with (an opinion) I *differ with* your views on public affairs.

discriminate against A white supremacist *discriminates against* virtually everybody.

dissuade from   She will *dissuade* him *from* making that poor investment.

distinguish from   I cannot *distinguish* one twin *from* the other.

employed at (a definite salary)   The student aide is *employed at* the minimum wage.

employed in (certain work)   His brother is *employed in* reading blueprints.

envious of   Some of the employees are *envious of* his good fortune.

escape from   I *escaped from* the prison by digging a hole through the wall.

excel in/at   I *excel in/at* all my academic subjects.

identical to/with   These stockings are *identical to/with* those I showed you last week.

in accordance with   Act *in accordance with* the regulations.

infer from   I *infer from* his remarks that he is dissatisfied.

inferior to   He feels *inferior to* his successful brother.

in regard to   This is a phone call *in regard to* your complaint.

insist on   I *insist on* helping you with this burden.

necessary to   Your help is *necessary to* the success of the project.

object to   Please do not *object to* my request.

oblivious of/to   The typist is *oblivious of/to* the construction noise outside.

opposite to/from   Your viewpoint is *opposite to/from* mine.

pertinent to   Your comment is not really *pertinent to* the discussion.

plan to   Do you *plan to* go to the play tonight?

prefer to   She *prefers* silk *to* polyester.

prevent from   I *prevented* her *from* falling by grabbing her shirt.

prohibit from   My parents *prohibit* me *from* smoking.

protect from   I shall *protect* you *from* him.

prior to   You will receive a deposit *prior to* the final settlement.

recover from   It took a long time for her to *recover from* her illness.

rely on   I *rely on* my parents for financial support.

required of   The letter states what is *required of* you.

stay at   He wants to *stay at* home this evening.

substitute for   There is no *substitute for* hard work.

succeed in   I have *succeeded in* accomplishing my goal.

susceptible to   She is not *susceptible to* even the deadliest of diseases.

try to   I will *try to* come on time.

vie with   The salesman are *vying with* one another for this week's prize.

Idioms Exercise

Complete each sentence with correct idiom.

1. I am concerned _____ the present state of the economy.

2. If you are so insistent, then I cannot dissuade you _____ your plans.

3. He lives _____ New Jersey.

4. He lives _____ the boarding house.

5. He lives _____ Broad Avenue.

6. We agreed _____ a fair divorce settlement.

7. He prefers sweaters _____ turtlenecks.

8. Your comments are not pertinent _____ our discussion.

9. We argued _____ the upcoming election all day.

10. I am confident _____ my ability to take the test.

11. The scantily clad woman was oblivious _____ the stares of the passerby.

12. My mother is employed as an editor _____ Random House publishing.

13. She was angry _____ her teacher for yelling at her in class.

14. Children rely _____ their parents for guidance.

15. The doctor is available _____ consultation this afternoon.

16. I am very adept _____ any sport that requires hand-eye coordination.

17. I plan _____ study my Achieve Academy grammar book every night

18. The gift was accompanied _____ a card.

19. In appearance fraternal twins are often very different _____ each other.

20. Although I will most likely be late, I will try _____ come on time.

 ## Double Negatives

A double negative consists of two negatives put together. Such phrasing is not allowed unless one word is meant to cancel out the other.

Bad	I cannot hardly sleep.
Good	I can hardly sleep.

Bad	Barely no one passed the test.
Good	Barely anyone passed the test.

Bad	There was scarcely no food.
Good	There was scarcely any food.

However, a phrase in which two negative words are meant to cancel each other out is not incorrect.

> • It is not uncommon these days to roller blade to work.

The only words you really have to watch out for in double negatives are: *hardly*, *barely*, and *scarcely*. Whenever you spot one of these words, check to see if it is a double negative.

 Double Negatives Exercise

 Correct any double negatives.

1. Until Copernicus proposed his theory, scarcely no one believed that the sun was the center of the universe.

2. The decline of outmoded industries has resulted in an unstable economy, since no easy way of retraining workers has never been found.

3. Many submarine volcanoes lie at such great depth that eruptions occur without hardly any release of gas or steam.

4. Charles Dickens had not written fiction for scarcely three years when he became a bestselling novelist.

5. Practically no big-time college football team has enjoyed success on the gridiron without increasing overall athletic department revenues.

6. Because consumer electronics are so affordable today, hardly no college student needs to go without a personal stereo.

7. Last summer's extended drought means there may not be scarcely enough wheat to satisfy the growing demand.

8. The author's latest work is so powerfully written and emotionally charged that hardly any commentators have criticized it.

9. Being pulled into the teenage social scene of drugs and underage drinking is not an unavoidable undertaking.

10. The rapacious pests had left barely nothing on the lettuce patch.

Part

2

SAT Ⅱ : Writing with Essay Workbook

SAT Ⅱ : Writing with Essay Workbook

SAT Ⅱ : Writing with Essay Workbook

SAT Ⅱ : Writing with Essay Workbook

SAT Ⅱ : Writing with Essay Workbook

SAT Ⅱ : Writing with Essay Workbook

SAT Ⅱ : Writing with Essay Workbook

SAT Ⅱ : Writing with Essay Workbook

SAT Ⅱ : Writing with Essay Workbook

SAT Ⅱ : Writing with Essay Workbook

SAT Ⅱ : Writing with Essay Workbook

SAT Ⅱ : Writing with Essay Workbook

SAT Ⅱ : Writing with Essay Workbook

SAT Ⅱ : Writing with Essay Workbook

Confused Words List 1

(a) **accept** means *to receive* or *to agree to* something

except means *to exclude* or *excluding*

> - Jane'll *accept* the gift from you.
> - Everyone *except* James went home.
> - Peter was *excepted* from the group of losers.

(a) **advice** means *counsel* (noun), *opinion*

advise means *to offer advice* (verb)

> - Let me give you some variable *advice*.
> - I'd *advise* her to see her teacher.

(a) **affect** means to *influence* (verb)

effect means *to cause* or *bring about* (verb) or *a result* (noun)

> - The pollution *affected* our health.
> - Our lawsuit *effected* a change in the law.
> - The *effect* of the storm could not be measured.

(a) **all ready** means *everybody* or *everything ready*

already means *previously*

> - They were *all ready* to write when the test began.
> - They had *already* written the essay.

all together means *everybody* or *everything together*

altogether means *completely*

> - The boys and girls stood *all together* in line.
> - His action was *altogether* strange for a person of his type.

desert [désəːrt] means a *dry area*

desert [dizə́ːrt] means *to abandon*, or a *reward or punishment* (usually plural)

dessert [dizə́ːrt] means *the final course of a meal*

> - I have seen several movies set in the Sahara *desert*.
> - The soldier was warned not to *desert* his company.
> - We're certain that execution is a just *desert* for his crime. He received his just *deserts*.
> - We had strawberry shortcake for *dessert*.

in is used to indicate *inclusion*, *location*, or *motion within limits*

into is used for *motion toward* one place *from* another

> - The pens are *in* the drawer.
> - I put the pens *into* the drawer.

it's is the contraction of *it is* or *it has*

its is a possessive pronoun meaning *belonging to it*

> - *It's* a very difficult assignment.
> - *It is* a very difficult assignment.
> - We tried to analyze *its* meaning.

lay means *to put*

lie means *to recline*

To lay		
Present	I lay	
Past	I laid	the gift on the table.
Present perfect	I have laid	

To lie		
Present	I lie	
Past	I lay	on my blanket at the beach.
Present perfect	I have lain	

lets is third person singular present of *let*

let's is a contradiction for *let us*

> • He *lets* me park my car in his garage.
> • *Let's* go home early today.

loose means *not fastened* or *restrained*, or *not tight-fitting*

lose means to *mislay, to be unable to keep, to be defeated*

> • The dog got *loose* from the leash.
> • Try not to *lose* your lighter.

principal means *chief* or *main* (adjective), or a *leader*, or a *sum of money* (noun)

principle means a *fundamental truth* or *belief*

> • His *principal* support comes from the stock market.
> • The *principal* of the school called a meeting of the faculty.
> • He earned 10% interest on the *principal* be invested last year.
> • As a matter of *principle*, he refused to give up his property.

raise means *to lift, to erect*

raze means *to tear down*

rise means *to get up, to move from a lower to a higher position, to increase in value.*

> - The neighbors helped him *raise* a new barn.
> - The demolition crew *razed* the old building.
> - The price of gold will *rise* again next month.

set means *to place something down* (mainly)

sit means *to seat oneself* (mainly)

To set		
Present	She sets	
Past	She set	the lamp on the table.
Present perfect	She has set	

To sit		
Present	She sits	
Past	She sat	on the chair.
Present perfect	She has sat	

stationary means *standing still*

stationery means *writing material*

> - In ancient times, people thought that the earth was *stationary*.
> - We bought our school supplies at the *stationery* store.

than is used to express *comparison*

then is used to express *time* or a *result* or *consequence*

> - Jim ate more *than* we could put on the large plate.
> - I knocked on the door, and *then* I entered.
> - If you leave, *then* I will leave, too.

their means *belonging to them*

there means *in that place*

they're is the contraction for *they are*

> - We took *their* magazines home with us.
> - Your magazines are over *there* on the desk.
> - *They're* coming over for dinner.

though means *although* or *as if*

thought is the past tense of *to think*, or *an idea* (noun)

through means *in one side and out another, by way of, finished*

> - *Though* Peter is my friend, I can't recommend him for this job.
> - I *thought* you were serious!
> - We enjoyed running *through* the rain.

to means *in the direction of* (preposition); it is also used before a verb to indicate the *infinitive*

too means *very, also*

two is the numeral *2*

> - We shall go *to* the party.
> - We shall go, *too*.
> - It is *too* cold today.
> - I ate *two* sandwiches for lunch.

were is a past tense of *be*

we're is a contraction of *we are*

where refers to *place* or *location*

> - They *were* there yesterday.
> - *We're* in charge of the decorations.
> - *Where* are we meeting your brother?

who's is the contraction for *who is* (or *who has*)

whose means *of whom*, implying ownership

> - *Who's* the next batter?
> - *Whose* wallet is on the table?

your is a possessive, showing ownership

you're is a contraction for *you are*

> - Please give him *your* notebook.
> - *You're* very sweet.

 Exercise 1

⬇ *Choose the correct word for each sentence.*

1. If (your, you're) tired, just (lay, lie) down for a while.

2. Do you think I will get (accepted, excepted) (in, into) the program?

3. I would (advice, advise) you to take your mother's (advice, advise).

4. The (affect, effect) of this storm will be devastating.

5. The soloist will finish her part, and then we will sing (all together, altogether).

6. This writing class is much more fun (than, then) I had imagined.

7. (Who's, Whose) pen is this?

8. I like to exercise in my basement on my (stationary, stationery) bike.

9. Every morning we (raise, raze, rise) the flag before the sun (raises, razes, rises).

10. What would you like for (desert, dessert)?

11. Don't (lose, loose) your ticket stub just in case the usher checks.

12. Give the dog (it's, its) bone.

13. The (principal, principle) issue at hand is the budget.

14. Is it (all ready, already) evening?

15. I managed to finish all my homework (though, thought, through) I was so sleepy.

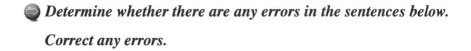
Exercise 2

➲ *Determine whether there are any errors in the sentences below. Correct any errors.*

1. Your shoelaces are loose.

2. Your opinion will not affect mine.

3. Were about to go to the theater, but we don't know were it is.

4. I want too go too the movies.

5. Everyone in school went on the trip except for me.

6. Your slice of pizza is bigger then mine.

7. Lay the baby down for a nap.

8. Let's go to the park after dinner.

9. Who's computer is that?

10. They're going to put on a skit for the Christmas pageant.

11. The evil man received a just desert when he was abandoned in the desert.

12. Its just a matter of time before we all die.

13. Her cat ran straight for it's bowl of food.

14. This is altogether too boring to read.

15. Have their been any calls for me?

Confused Words List 2

allusion means *an indirect reference*

illusion means *an false concept or false perception*

> - The poem contains an *allusion* to one of Shakespeare's sonnets.
> - The mirror created the *illusion* of space in the narrow hall.

allude means *to make a reference to*

elude means *to escape from*

> - In his essay, he *alludes* to Shakespeare's puns.
> - The burglar *eluded* the police.

breath means *an intake of air*

breathe means *to draw air in and let it out*

breadth means *width*

> - Before you dive in, take a very deep *breath*.
> - It is sometimes difficult to *breathe* when you have a bad cold.
> - The artist's canvas was twice greater in length than in *breadth*.

build means *to erect, construct* (verb), or the *physical form* of a person or thing (noun)

built is the past tense of *build*

> - I want to *build* a sand castle.
> - She has a very athletic *build*.
> - We *built* a moat around the sand castle.

capital refers to the *place of government* or to *wealth*

capitol refers to the *building* which houses the state or national legislatures

> - Paris is the *capital* of France.
> - It takes substantial *capital* to open a restaurant.
> - Congress convenes in the *Capitol* in Washington, D.C.

choice means a *selection*

choose means *to select*

chose is the *past tense of choose*

> - My *choice* for a career is teaching.
> - We may *choose* our own advisors.
> - I finally *chose* my wedding dress.

cite means *to quote*

sight means *seeing, what is seen*

site means a *place where something is located or occurs*

> - He enjoys *citing* Shakespeare to illustrate his views.
> - The *sight* of the accident was appalling.
> - We are seeking a new *site* for the baseball field.

cloth is *fabric* or *material*

clothe means *to put on clothes, to dress*

> • The seats were covered with *cloth*, not vinyl.
> • Her job is to *clothe* the actors for each scene.

complement means *a completing part*

compliment is *an expression of praise or admiration* (something given without charge is *complimentary*)

> • His wit was a *complement* to her beauty.
> • He received many *compliments* for his fine work.

conscience refers to the ability to *recognize the difference between right and wrong*

conscious means *aware*

> • The attorney claimed that the criminal lacked a *conscience*.
> • He was *conscious* that his action would have serious consequences.

consul means a *government representative*

council means an *assembly that meets for deliberation* (councilor)

counsel means *advice* (counselor)

> • Americans abroad should keep in touch with their *consuls*.
> • The student *council* met to discuss a campus dress code.
> • The defendant heeded the *counsel* of his friends.

🔒 **decent** means *suitable*

descent means *going down*

dissent means *disagreement*

> - The *decent* thing to do is to admit your error.
> - The *descent* into the cave was dangerous.
> - Two of the justices filed a *dissenting* opinion.

🔒 **farther** is preferred to express *distance*

further is preferred to express *time or degree*

> - John ran *farther* than Bill walked.
> - Please go no *further* in your argument.

🔒 **later** means *after a certain time*

latter means *the second of two*

> - I'll see you *later*.
> - Of the two speakers, the *latter* was more interesting.

🔒 **moral** means *good or ethical* (adjective) or a *lesson to be drawn* (noun)

morale (more-AL) means *spirit*

> - The administrator of the trust had a *moral* obligation to the heirs.
> - The *moral* of the story is that it pays to be honest.
> - The *morale* of the team improved after the coach's half-time speech.

🔒 **personal** refers to an *individual's character, conduct, private affairs*

personnel means an *organized body of individuals*

> • The professor took a *personal* interest in each of his graduate students.
> • The store's *personnel* department is on the third floor.

Exercise 1

🖊 *Choose the correct word for each sentence below.*

1. Is your (conscience, conscious) bothering you?

2. This is a (personal, personnel) matter that I would like to handle privately.

3. It's good to use (allusions, illusions) in your essays.

4. We should give the chef a (complement, compliment) for this delicious meal.

5. I prefer the (later, latter) to the former.

6. I need some more (capital, capitol) to start my new business.

7. Contrary to popular belief, Rome was not (build, built) in a day.

8. The criminal tried vainly to (allude, elude) the police.

9. I cannot (breath, breathe) when I have a stuffy nose.

10. You should always (cite, site) references made in your papers.

11. I shall (choose, chose) the prettiest for my bride.

12. The devastating failure dropped the team's (moral, morale).

13. The airplane's sharp (decent, descent) popped my ears.

14. My (council, counsel) shall represent me in court.

15. The store is much (farther, further) than you think.

Exercise 2

Determine if there is an error in any of the sentences below. Correct any errors.

1. I would like to visit the capital of the United States.

2. What is the morale of this story?

3. Isn't she a pretty site?

4. Before you pointed it out to me, I had not been conscious of my fidgeting.

5. I will do my chores latter, when I have time.

6. The table was draped with gingham cloth.

7. I need more personnel to help with the holiday work load.

8. Red wine compliments steak better than white wine does.

9. I have sent my consul to discuss this matter with you privately.

10. If no one dissents, we shall begin voting on this issue.

11. I couldn't catch my breadth after running so fast.

12. Which Greek myth are you alluding to?

13. I need to site a reference book for my research paper.

14. I do not understand why people clothe their dogs.

15. The people of this community are hard-working and decent.

Confused Words List 3

accede means *to agree with*

exceed means *to be more than*

concede means *to yield* (not necessarily in agreement)

> - They will *accede* to your request for more information.
> - Unfortunately, her expenditures now *exceed* her income.
> - To avoid delay, they will *concede* that more information is necessary.

access means *availability*

excess means *the state of surpassing specified limits* (noun) or *more than usual* (adjective)

> - The lawyer was given *access* to the grand jury records.
> - Expenditures this month are far in *excess* of income.
> - The airlines charged him fifty dollars for *excess* baggage.

adapt means *to adjust or change*

adept means *skillful*

adopt means *to take as one's own*

> - Children can *adapt* to changing conditions very easily.
> - Proper instruction makes children *adept* in various games.
> - The war orphan was *adopted* by the general and his wife.

adverse means *unfavorable*

averse means *having a feeling of repugnance* or *dislike*

> • He was very upset by the *adverse* decision.
> • Many writers are *averse* to criticism of their work.

canvas is a *heavy, coarse material*

canvass means *to solicit, conduct a survey*

> • The *canvas* sails were very heavy.
> • The local politicians are going to *canvass* our neighborhoods.

carat is a *unit of weight*

caret is a *proofreading symbol*, indicating where something is to be inserted

carrot is a *vegetable*

> • The movie star wears a ten-*carat* diamond ring.
> • He added a phrase in the space above the *caret*.
> • Does he feed his pet rabbit a *carrot* every other day?

click is a *brief, sharp sound*

clique is an *exclusive group of people*, a *circle*, or *set*

> • The detective drew his gun when he heard the *click* of the lock.
> • In high school, I was not part of any *clique*.

confidant is *one to whom private matters are confided* (noun)

confident means *being sure, having confidence in oneself* (adjective)

confidence a *feeling of assurance or certainty, trust* (noun)

> - His priest was his only *confidant.*
> - Her success in business has given her a very *confident* manner.
> - The ballplayer is developing *confidence* in his fielding ability.

disburse means *to pay out*

disperse means *to scatter*, *distribute widely*

> - This week the bank has *disbursed* a million dollars.
> - The defeated army began to *disperse*.

discomfit means *to upset*

discomfort means *lack of ease*

> - The general's plan was designed to *discomfit* the enemy.
> - This starched collar causes *discomfort.*

elicit means *to draw forth*, *evoke*

illicit means *illegal*, *unlawful*

> - Her performance *elicited* tears from the audience.
> - He was arrested because of his *illicit* business dealings.

emigrate means *to leave a country*

immigrate means *to enter a country*

> - The Norwegians *emigrated* to the United States in the nineteenth century.
> - Many of the Norwegian *immigrants* settled in the Midwest.

eminent means *of high rank, prominent, outstanding*

imminent means *about to occur, impending*

> • He was the most *eminent* physician of his time.
> • His nomination to the board of directors is *imminent*.

epitaph is a *memorial inscription on a tombstone* or *monument*

epithet is a *term used to describe* or *characterize the nature of a person or thing*

> • His *epitaph* was taken from a section of the Bible.
> • The drunk was shouting *epithets* and being abusive to passerby.

expand means *to spread out*

expend means *to use up*

> • As the staff increases, we can *expand* our office space.
> • Don't *expend* all your energy on one project.

formally means *in a formal way*

formerly means *at an earlier time*

> • He was dressed *formally* for the dinner party.
> • He was *formerly* a delegate to the convention.

fort means a fortified place

forte [fɔːrt] means a strong point

forte [fɔːrtei] is a musical term that means loudly

> • A small garrison was able to hold the *fort*.
> • Conducting Wagner's music was Toscanini's *forte*.
> • The final movement of the musical composition was meant to be played *forte*.

incidence refers to *the extent* or *frequency of an occurrence*

incidents refers to *occurrences, events*

> • The *incidence* of rabies has decreased since the beginning of the year.
> • Luckily, the accidents were just minor *incidents*.

 prophecy means *prediction* (noun, rhymes with sea)

prophesy means *to predict* (verb, rhymes with sigh)

> • What is the fortune-teller's *prophecy*?
> • What did the witches *prophesy*?

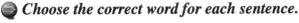

Exercise 1

🔽 *Choose the correct word for each sentence.*

1. The school does not sanction the sale of (elicit, illicit) drugs.

2. Ansel Adams is an (eminent, imminent) photographer of nature scenes.

3. The soothsayer's (prophecy, prophesy) came true on the Ides of March.

4. Every masterpiece begins as a blank (canvas, canvass).

5. I am (confidant, confident) that the other party will agree to the deal.

6. This pen is plated with 14 (carat, caret) gold.

7. I hope I do not suffer any (averse, adverse) effects from the experimental drug.

8. The price of a product should not (accede, exceed) its quality.

9. In this school every (click, clique) of friends is very exclusive.

10. I (emigrated, immigrated) from South Korea when I was barely three.

11. The police attempted to (disburse, disperse) the mob quietly.

12. The old wooden chair gave me a great deal of (discomfit, discomfort).

13. On my (epitaph, epithet) it shall read, "R.I.P."

14. We shall (expand, expend) all our energy on this project till we are done.

15. Piano-playing is not my (fort, forte).

 Exercise 2

🡆 *Determine if there are any errors in the sentences below. Correct all errors.*

1. The creature has adopted to its new environment very well.

2. The incidence of malaria is very high in the southern provinces.

3. We should close the window, for the storm is eminent.

4. Each party discussed the most efficient ways to canvas its voting district.

5. Though my name is Joe Park, I was formally known as Hitler in my past life.

6. The crowd flung harsh epithets at the death row inmate.

7. A loud-mouth does not make a good confidant.

8. Insert a caret wherever you accidentally omitted a word.

9. Since I am a neat freak, I am very adverse to any sort of mess.

10. I do not believe that fortune tellers have any power to prophecy.

11. A town curfew is in effect because of the recent rash of riotous incidence.

12. The poor comedian was not able to elicit any laughter from the stern audience.

13. The forte was garrisoned with heavily armed soldiers.

14. Please dress formally for the occasion.

15. Give the carrot to the donkey.

Confused Words List 4

abbreviate means *to shorten by omitting*

abridge means *to shorten by condensing*

> - New York is *abbreviated* to NY.
> - In order to save time in the reading, the report was *abridged*.

advantage means *a superior position*

benefit means *a favor conferred or earned* (as a profit)

> - He had an *advantage* in experience over his opponent.
> - The rules were changed for his *benefit*.

aggravate means *to make worse*

annoy means *to bother* or *to irritate*

> - Your nasty comments *aggravated* a bad situation.
> - Your nasty comments *annoyed* him.(Not: Your nasty comments aggravated him.)

all ways means *in every possible way*

always means *at all times*

> - He was in *all ways* acceptable to the voters.
> - He was *always* ready to help.

allot means *to give* or *apportion*

> • I will *allot* three hours for painting the table.

alot is a misspelling of *a lot*

> • He earned *a lot* of money. (better: He earned *a great deal* of money.)

alright is now often employed in common usage to mean all right (In formal usage all right is still preferred by most authorities.)
all right means satisfactory, very well, uninjured, or without doubt

> • I'm *alright*, thank you.
> • It was his responsibility, *all right*.

alternate, as a noun, means *a substitute* or *second choice*
alternate, as a verb, means *to perform by turns*
alternative means *a choice between two things, only one of which may be accepted*

> • She served as an *alternate* delegate to the convention.
> • The cook *alternated* green beans and cauliflower on the menu.
> • Is there an *alternative* to the proposition?

alumna means *a female graduate* (plural: alumnae; ae rhymes with key)
alumnus means *a male graduate* (plural: alumni; ni rhymes with high)

> • She is an *alumna* of Mrs. Brown's School for Young Women.
> • He is an *alumnus* of City College.

🔒 **among** is used to discuss *more than two* items

between is used to discuss *two* items only

> • The work was divided *among* the four brothers.
> • She divided the pie *between* Joe and Marie.

🔒 **amount** is used to refer to *a quantity not individually countable*

number is used to refer to *items that can be counted individually*

> • A tremendous *amount* of work had piled up on my desk.
> • We ate a great *number* of cookies at the party.

🔒 **annual** means *yearly*

biannual means *twice a year* (also *semiannual*)

biennial means *once in two years or every two years*

> • Are you going to the *annual* holiday party?
> • I receive *biannual* statements concerning my automobile insurance in April and in October.
> • He gets a new car *biennially*.

🔒 **anxious** means *worried*

eager means *keenly desirous*

> • We were *anxious* about our first airplane flight.
> • I am *eager* to see you again.

🔒 **aren't I** is used informally, but in formal usage *am I not* is correct

> • *Am I not* entitled to an explanation?

🔒 **around** should not be used in formal writing as a substitute for *about* or *near*

> • I'll be there about (not around) 2 P.M.

🔒 **as** is not always as clear as *because*, *for*, or *since* (also see like)

> • She wants to cry *because* she is very sad.

🔒 **as** used as a *conjunction*, is followed by a verb
like used as a *preposition*, is not followed by a verb

> • Do *as* I do, not *as* I say.
> • Try not to behave *like* a child.

🔒 **as...as** is used in an *positive* comparison
so...as is used in a *negative* comparison

> • She is *as* talented *as* any other actress in the show.
> • He is not *so* reliable *as* his older brother.

🔒 **astonish** means *to strike with sudden wonder*
surprise means *to catch unaware*

> • The extreme violence of the hurricane *astonished* everybody.
> • A heat wave in April would *surprise* us.

🔒 **bad** is used after verbs that refer to the senses, such as *look*, *feel* (adjective)
badly means *greatly*, *in a bad manner* (adverb)

> • He felt *bad* that he could not attend the meeting.
> • The young man needs a part-time job very *badly*.

being as and *being that* is incorrect. Use *because* and *since*.

> - *Since* it was dark, we turned on the lights.
> - *Because* he is my friend, I gave him a gift.

Exercise 1

◉ *Choose the correct word for each sentence.*

1. Please divide the pizza evenly (among, between) the three of you.

2. Mrs. Brown is an (alumna, alumnus) of Columbia University.

3. Being a minority these days often gives you an added (advantage, benefit) over everyone else.

4. I feel (bad, badly) for running over her dog.

5. The (amount, number) of people at the concert was amazing.

6. Your constant pestering is beginning to (aggravate, annoy) me.

7. I am very (anxious, eager) about the upcoming examination.

8. The (annual, biannual) picnic comes but once a year.

9. The boy who sprang out of the bushes (astonished, surprised) me.

10. I (always, all ways) want to be with you.

11. (Because, Being as) it is raining, we will cancel the game.

12. It is customary to (abbreviate, abridge) state names to their initials.

13. I have done (a lot, allot) of the work while you were gone.

14. Do you know an (alternate, alternative) route to our destination?

15. I will be there (about, around) 5 o'clock.

➡ *Determine if there are any errors in the sentences below. Correct all errors.*

1. "Aren't I" is the correct contraction for "are I not."

2. I got all the answers on my test alright.

3. I am as good as you are at skeet shooting.

4. However, I am not as good as you are at archery.

5. I am very eager to begin at my new workplace.

6. We should be able to complete the work if we split it among the four of us.

7. I want to be as Mike.

8. He has been cooperative in all ways.

9. This coffee tastes very bad.

10. Though there is a lot of traffic on the main route, there is no alternate way to my house.

11. The natural phenomenon of the Aurora Borealis astonished the audience.

12. If it is alright with you, I would like to go home.

13. The Tylenol will only aggravate your stomach pains.

14. You are very bad at sports.

15. I will be late, as I will be coming from the airport.

Confused Words List 5

bring means *to carry toward the speaker*

take means *to carry away from the speaker*

> - *Bring* the coat to me.
> - *Take* money for carfare when you leave.

bunch should be used to describe a group of objects. Use *group* to describe a group of people

> - When he returned to his office, he learned that a *group* of students was waiting for him.

can means *able*

may implies *permission* or *possibility*

> - I *can* eat both desserts.
> - *May* I eat both desserts?
> - It *may* snow tonight.

consistently means *in harmony*

constantly means *regularly*, *steadily*

> - If you give me advice, you should act *consistently* with that advice.
> - I *constantly* warned him about leaving the door unlocked.

ⓐ **could of** is an incorrect form of *could have*

> • I wish that I *could have* gone.

ⓐ **couple** refers to *two*, *several* or *a few* refers to more than two

> • Alex and Frieda are the most graceful *couple* on the dance floor.
> • *A few* of my cousins-Mary, Margie, Alice, and Barbara-will be at the reunion tonight.

ⓐ **data** is the Latin plural of datum, meaning *information* (*data* is preferred with plural verbs and pronouns, but is now acceptable in the singular)

> • *These data* were very significant to the study. (or *This data* was very significant to the study.)

ⓐ **different than** is incorrect. Use *different from*

> • Jack is *different from* his brother.

ⓐ **disinterested** means *impartial*
uninterested means *not interested*

> • The judge must be a *disinterested* party in a trial.
> • I'm an *uninterested* bystander, so I find the proceedings boring.

ⓐ **doubt whether** is incorrect. Use *doubt that*

> • I *doubt that* I will be home this evening.

ⓘ **due to** can only be used following a conjugated form of the "to be" verb. Thus, *due to* should never start a sentence to substitute for *because of*

> • *Because of* (not *due to*) the rain, the game was postponed. (but: The postponement was *due to* the rain.)

ⓘ **each other** refers to *two persons*
one another refers to *more than two persons*

> • Jane and Jessica have known *each other* for many years.
> • Several of the girls have known *one another* for many years.

ⓘ **else than** is incorrect. Use *other than*

> • Shakespeare was rarely regarded by students as anything *other than* the writer of plays.

ⓘ **enthuse** or *enthused* should be avoided; use *enthusiastic*

> • We were *enthusiastic* when given the chance to travel abroad.

ⓘ **equally as good** is an incorrect form; *equally good* or *just as good* is correct

> • This bicycle is *just as good* as that one.

ⓘ **etc.** is the abbreviation for the Latin term *et cetera*, meaning *and so forth*, *and other things*. Don't use it in formal writing. Instead, just list several examples using *such as*, to imply that what you list are only examples and not everything.

> • I like sports, *such as* basketball, baseball and badminton.

🔒 **everyone**, written as one word, is a *pronoun*

every one, written as two words, is used to refer to *each individual*

> • *Everyone* present voted for the proposal.
> • *Every one* of the voters accepted the proposal.

🔒 **expect** does not mean *assume* or *presume*

> • I *assume* (not *expect*) that he won the race.

Exercise 1

🔘 *Choose the correct word for each sentence.*

1. I picked a large (bunch, group) of grapes off the vine.

2. My handwriting is very different (from, than) yours.

3. Will you (bring, take) this with you to the library?

4. I doubt (that, whether) it will snow today because it's so warm.

5. I am very (enthused, enthusiastic) about our upcoming pool party.

6. I (assume, expect) that you will be punctual this time.

7. A judge should remain (disinterested, uninterested) during a trial.

8. (Can, May) I go to the party today?

9. The phone has been ringing (consistently, constantly) ever since we won the lottery.

10. The various data for this experiment (are, is) not all gathered.

11. I could (have, of) won the contest if I had tried harder.

12. (Because of, Due to) the rain, the game will be cancelled.

13. Flopsy, Mopsy and Benjamin Bunny have known (each other, one another) for a very long time.

14. (Everyone, Every one) of the students was absent from class today.

15. I am (equally as good, just as good) of a singer as you are.

Exercise 2

Determine if there are any errors in the sentences below. Correct all errors.

1. I am very uninterested by your lectures on paleobotany.

2. The two talked to each other all day on the phone.

3. I have performed consistently on my achievement tests.

4. Everyone is going to the musical tonight.

5. We are going to have to take another flight on account of the weather.

6. I dislike all insects-ants, cockroaches, flies, etc.

7. Can you assist me with this transaction?

8. I doubt that she will come on time.

9. There was a bunch of people waiting on line.

10. My car is equally as good as the one he wants to sell me.

11. The four partners of the firm have all worked with each other on several occasions.

12. Every one of the celebrities was dressed to impress.

13. May I borrow your phone?

14. Bring your books with you to class.

15. It rained constantly yesterday.

Confused Words List 6

fewer is used to refer to items that can be counted

less is used to refer to something viewed as a mass, not as a series of individual items

> • I made *fewer* repairs on the new car than on the old one.
> • After the scandal, the company enjoyed *less* prestige than it had the previous year.

finalized does not mean *completed*. Use *completed*

> • Labor and management completed arrangements for a settlement.

flaunt means *to make a display of*

flout means *to show contempt, scorn*

> • He *flaunted* his new wealth in an ostentatious manner.
> • She *flouted* the policeman's authority.

former means *the first of two*

latter means *the second of two*

> • The *former* half of the story was in prose.
> • The *latter* half of the story was in poetry.

🔒 **good** is an adjective; *well* is an adverb

> • She is a *good* singer.
> • She sings *well*.

🔒 **graduated** is followed by the preposition *from* when it indicates completion of a course of study
graduated also means *divided into categories* or *marked intervals*

> • He *graduated from* high school last year. (or: He was *graduated from* high school last year.)
> • A *graduated* test tube is one that has markings on it to indicate divisions.

🔒 **guess** should not be used to substitute for *think* or *suppose*

> • I *think* (not *guess*) I'll go home now.

🔒 **habit** means *an individual tendency to repeat a thing*
custom means *group habit*

> • He had a *habit* of breaking glasses before each recital.
> • The *custom* of the country was to betroth girls at an early age.

🔒 **hanged** is used in reference to a *person*
hung is used in reference to a *thing*

> • The prisoner was *hanged* in the town square.
> • The drapes were *hung* unevenly.

🔒 **healthful** is used to express whatever *gives* health
healthy is used to express whatever *has* health

> • He follows a *healthful* diet.
> • He is a *healthy* person.

hisself is a misspelling of *himself*

> • Let him do it *himself*.

human is an adjective and should always be followed by a noun. Never say *humans*

> • He says that love is a basic need of all *human beings*.
> • He says that love is a basic *human* need.

if introduces a *condition*

whether introduces a *choice*

> • I shall go to Greece *if* I win the prize.
> • He asked me *whether* I intended to go to Greece.

if it was implies that *something might have been true in the past*

if it were implies *doubt* or indicates *something that is contrary to fact*

> • *If* your book *was* there last night, it is there now.
> • *If it were* summer now, we would all go swimming.

imply means *to suggest or hint at* (the speaker *implies*)

infer means *to deduce or conclude* (the listener *infers*)

> • Are you *implying* that I have disobeyed orders?
> • From your carefree tone, what else are we to *infer*?

in regards to is an incorrect form for *in regard to*

> • He called me *in regard to* your letter.

🔒 **instance where** is incorrect. Use *instance in which*

> • Can you tell me of one *instance in which* such a terrible thing occurred?

🔒 **irregardless** is an incorrect form for *regardless*

> • I'll be your friend *regardless* of what people say, even if the people are accurate.

🔒 **is when** and **is where** are incorrect. Use *occurs when* and *is a place*

> • The best scene *occurs when* the audience least expects it.
> • My favorite vacation spot is *a place* where there are no telephones.

🔒 **kind of** and **sort of** are informal expressions that should be rephrased in formal writing-for instance, *somewhat* or *rather* are preferable

> • I am *rather* sorry he retired.
> • He was *somewhat* late for the meeting.

🔒 **lend** is a verb meaning *to give to*

loan is a noun denoting *what is given*

borrow means *to take from*

> • The bank was willing to *lend* him $500.
> • He was granted a *loan* of $500.
> • I'd like to *borrow* your electric drill for an hour.

🔒 **liable** means *responsible according to the law*

likely suggests *probable behavior*

> - If he falls down the stairs, we may be *liable* for damages.
> - A cat, if annoyed, is *likely* to scratch.

libel is a *written and published statement injurious to a person's character*

slander is a *spoken statement of the same sort*

> - The unsubstantiated negative comments about me in your book constitute *libel.*
> - When you say these vicious things about me, you are committing *slander.*

like is a preposition used to *introduce a phrase*

as if is used to *introduce a clause (a subject and a verb)*

as is a conjunction used to *introduce a clause*

like if is an incorrect form for *like*, *as*, or *as if*

> - It seems *like* a sunny day.
> - It seems *as if* it is going to be a sunny day.
> - He acted *as* he was expected to act.

many refers to *a number*

much refers to *a quantity* or *amount*

> - How *many* inches of rain fell last night?
> - *Much* rain fell last night.

may of is an incorrect for *may have*

might of is an incorrect form for *might have*

> - He *may have* been there, but I didn't see him.
> - I *might have* gone to the party if I hadn't been ill.

● *Choose the correct word for each sentence.*

1. There are (fewer, less) people in this room than in that room.

2. (Human beings, Humans) are the smartest beings on earth.

3. I prefer the (farmer, former) to the (later, latter).

4. (Many, Much) effort goes into baking a cake.

5. It is my daily (custom, habit) to brush my teeth.

6. I can (imply, infer) the author's tone from the passage.

7. You act (as if, like) I should be bothered by your retort.

8. I am calling (in regard to, in regards to) your letter.

9. I am going to Great Adventure (irregardless, regardless) of the weather.

10. The man was (hanged, hung) in the execution square today.

11. I will (graduate, graduate from) high school in just a few months.

12. This salad is very (healthful, healthy).

13. I did not feel (good, well) after eating the hot dog.

14. I will (lend, loan) you the money that you need.

15. Criminals love to (flaunt, flout) the law.

Determine if there are any errors in the sentences below. Correct all errors.

1. I guess I will be there tomorrow.

2. The plans for the ski trip have been finalized.

3. Please tell me an instance where something like that could actually happen.

4. The newspaper was sued for libel.

5. I am kind of tired after that long run.

6. Swimming is when you get into the water and flail your arms and legs about you.

7. If it were snowing yesterday, there might be ice on the ground today.

8. If I was a rich man, I would buy a mall.

9. It is likely that the criminal will be convicted of all the charges.

10. The stupid man hit hisself on the head with the hammer.

11. Much leaves have fallen from the trees.

12. I hung my coat on the hanger.

13. The most exciting part of the film is when he races his enemy.

14. I have fewer toes on my right foot than on my left foot.

15. Humans are bad.

Confused Words List 7

○ **media** is the Latin plural of *medium*; it refers to a means of mass communication or artistic expression and is used with a plural verb
must of is incorrect form for *must have*

> • I *must have* been sleeping when you called. (A contraction of this term is unacceptable in formal usage.)

○ **myself** is used as an *intensifier* if the subject of the verb is *I*
myself, instead of *I* or *me*, is not correct

> • Since I know *myself* better, let me try it my way.
> • My daughter and *I* (not *myself*) will play.
> • They gave my son and *me* (not *myself*) some food.

○ **nice** should not be used to mean *pleasing*, *good*, *fine*; use a more specific word

> • This is a *sunny* (or *good* or *fine*) weather (not *nice* weather).
> • He is a *good* (or *kind*) person.

○ **off of** is incorrect; use *off*

> • Joe was taken *off of* the team. (correct: Joe was taken *off* the team.)

ⓐ **okay** should not be used. Use *good*, *satisfactory* or *acceptable*

> - Informal: His work is *okay*.
> - Formal: His work is *acceptable* (or *good*).

ⓐ **on account of** is an incorrect form for *because*

> - We could not meet you *because* we did not receive your message in time.

ⓐ **oral** means *spoken*

verbal means *expressed in words*, either spoken or written

> - Instead of writing a note, she gave him an *oral* message.
> - Shorthand must usually be transcribed into *verbal* form.

ⓐ **owing to** is incorrect; use *because*

> - *Because* of a change of management, his company cancelled the takeover attempt.

ⓐ **plan on** is incorrect; use *plan to*

> - Do you *plan to go* (not *plan on going*) to the lecture?

ⓐ **prefer ... than** and **prefer ... over** is incorrect form for *prefer ... to*

> - I should *prefer that to* anything else you might suggest.

ⓐ **quit** is not a substitute for *stop*

> - Please *stop* your complaining.

ⓐ **reason is because** is incorrect; use *the reason is that* or *because*

> • The *reason* she calls *is that* (not *because*) she is lonely. (or, She calls *because* she is lonely.)

🔒 **refer back/report back**: since *re* means *back* or *again*, the word *back* is redundant and should be omitted

> • Please *refer* to your notes.
> • Please *report* to the supervisor.

🔒 **repeat again** or **reiterate again** is redundant; *again* should be omitted

> • Please *repeat* (or *reiterate*) the instructions.

🔒 **respectfully** means *with respect and decency*

respectively means *as relating to each, in the order given*

> • The students listened *respectfully* to the principal.
> • Jane and Lena are the daughters *respectively* of Mrs. Smith and Mrs. Jones.

🔒 **run** should not be used to mean *conduct, manage*

> • He wants to *conduct* (not *run*) the operation on a profitable basis.

🔒 **same as** is an incorrect form for *in the same way as* or *just as*

> • The owner's son was treated *in the same way as* any other worker.

Exercise 1

Choose the correct word for each sentence.

1. I could not see anything (because of, owing to) the blackout.

2. I prefer purple things (over, to) blue things.

3. My father and (I, myself) will pack the bags.

4. The media (are, is) having a great time covering the election melee.

5. I will go to the park and take advantage of this (nice, pleasant) day.

6. The reason I quit my job is (because, that) I found it unfulfilling.

7. I must (have, of) dropped my wallet by the car.

8. I am going to have to (refer, refer back) to my notes.

9. Their (oral, verbal) presentation was excellent.

10. I plan (on, to) going to the mall later.

11 Please get (off, off of) the grass.

12. My uncle (manages, runs) a textile factory in Honduras.

13. Donna and Ronna are Mrs. Lim's and Mrs. Kim's daughters, (respectfully, respectively).

14. I think I should (quit, stop) smoking.

15. If your work is (okay, satisfactory), you will receive a B.

Determine if there are any errors in the sentences below. Correct all errors.

1. I have my subordinates report back to me every hour.

2. I hope you'll be able to repeat your marvelous performance again.

3. Are the media covering the local elections?

4. She studied the same as her friend, but she did worse.

5. I plan to join the orchestra this year.

6. If you are confused, please refer back to the instructions.

7. I treat both Mr. Park and Mr. Dark respectfully.

8. The reason you failed is because you didn't study.

9. I prefer cats over dogs.

10. She is such a nice person.

11. The SAT consists of math and verbal sections.

12. In rehearsal, she never even referred back to the script.

13. I will not repeat myself again.

14. Does he run the company efficiently?

15. We were unable to acquit him of the charges on account of the overwhelming evidence against him.

Confused Words List 8

🔒 **shape** is incorrect when used to mean *state* or *condition*

> • The refugees were in a *serious condition* (not *shape*) when they arrived here.

🔒 **should of** is an incorrect form for *should have*

> • You *should have* returned that sweater.

🔒 **sink down** is incorrect; *down* is redundant and should be omitted.

> • You can *sink* into the mud if you are not careful.

🔒 **some time** means *a segment of time*
sometime means *at an indefinite time in the future*
sometimes means *occasionally*

> • I'll need *some time* to make a decision.
> • Let's meet *sometime* next week.
> • *Sometimes* I have an urge to watch a late movie on television.

🔒 **testimony** means *information given orally*
evidence means *information given orally or in writing*; an *object* which is presented as proof

> - He gave *testimony* to the grand jury.
> - He presented written *evidence* to the judge.

🔒 **the both** is incorrect; omit *the*

> - I intend to treat *both* of you to lunch.

🔒 **their**, in informal usage, often appears in the construction "Anyone can lose their card," but since *anyone* takes a singular personal pronoun, *his* is the correct form

theirselves is an incorrect form for *themselves*

> - They are able to care for *themselves* while their parents are at work.

🔒 **try and** is incorrect; use *try to*

> - My acting teacher is going to *try to* attend the opening of my play.

🔒 **unbeknownst to** is unacceptable for *without the knowledge of*

> - The young couple decided to get married *without the knowledge of* (not *unbeknownst to*) their parents.

🔒 **valuable** means *of great worth*

valued means *held in high regard*

invaluable means *priceless*

> - This is a *valuable* manuscript.
> - You are a *valued* friend.
> - A good name is an *invaluable* possession.

🔒 **which** is sometimes used incorrectly to refer to *people*; it refers to *things*

who is used to refer to *people*

that is used to refer to *people* or *things*

> • He finally returned the books *which* he had borrowed.
> • I am looking for the girl *who* made the call.
> • He finally returned the books *that* he had borrowed.
> • I am looking for the girl *that* made the call.

🔒 **while** is unacceptable for *and*, *but*, *whereas*, or *though*

> • The library is situated on the south side, *whereas* (not *while*) the laboratory is on the north side.
> • *Though* (not *while*) I disagree with you, I shall not interfere with your right to express your opinion.

🔒 **who is**, **who am**-Note these constructions:

> • It is *I* who *am* the most experienced.
> • It is *he* who *is* ...
> • It is *he* or *I* who *am* ...
> • It is *I* or *he* who *is* ...
> • It is *he* and *I* who *are* ...

🔒 **who, whom**-To determine whether to use *who* or *whom* (without grammar rules): (*Who, Whom*) do you think should represent our company?

(1) Change the *who-whom* part of the sentence to its natural order:

> Do you think (*who, whom*) should represent our company?

(2) Substitute *he* for *who*, and *him* for *whom*:

> Do you think (*he, him*) should represent our company?

(3) Since *he* would be used in this case, the correct form is:

> *Who* do you think should represent our company?

🔒 ***whoever, whomever*** (see *who, whom* above)

> • Give the chair to *whoever* wants it (subject of verb *wants*).
> • Speak to *whomever* you see (object of preposition *to*).

🔒 ***would of*** is an incorrect form for *would have*

> • He *would have* treated you to the movies.

🔒 ***would have*** is *not* used instead of *had* in an *if* clause: If I *had* (not *would have*) gone, I would have helped him.

✏️ **Exercise 1**

📝 *Choose the correct word for each sentence.*

1. The nation's economy is in poor (condition, shape).

2. I should (have, of) done it when I had the chance.

3. It has been (some time, sometime) since I have read that novel.

4. The witness gave (evidence, testimony) in court yesterday.

5. I will try (and, to) do my best.

6. The person (which, who) took the keys will return them later.

7. The east side of campus is rural, (whereas, while) the west side is urban.

8. It is he or I who (am, is, are) going to the conference.

9. Do you know (who, whom) I should give this to?

10. I would (have, of) done the right thing if I weren't such a coward.

11. (Whoever, Whomever) used the stove last should also clean it.

12. If I (had, would have) known what was going to happen, I would have not shot the gun.

13. Instead of waiting for their ride, they decided to drive (theirselves, themselves).

14. (Sometime, sometimes) when I am upset, I eat an entire box of cookies.

15. To say love is (invaluable, valuable) means that it is imperfect.

Exercise 2

Determine if there are any errors in the sentences below. Correct all errors.

1. My room is very neat while yours is very messy.

2. After it hit the iceberg, the Titanic began to sink down to the bottom of the sea.

3. I will deal with the both of you later.

4. I should have been more careful as I was backing out of the driveway.

5. Whom will cook dinner tonight?

6. I will try and be more studious from now on.

7. Give the award to whomever you think deserves it.

8. This jewel is very invaluable.

9. It is he who is going to walk the dog.

10. That is the cat who ripped up my tie.

11. I would have been hurt if I hadn't jumped out of the way in time.

12. The shape of the house is like a pentagon.

13. I like ziti whereas Kitty likes cat food.

14. With whom are you going to the prom?

Appendix

SAT II : Writing with Essay Workbook

SAT II : Writing with Essay Workbook

SAT II : Writing with Essay Workbook

SAT II : Writing with Essay Workbook

SAT II : Writing with Essay Workbook

SAT II : Writing with Essay Workbook

SAT II : Writing with Essay Workbook

SAT II : Writing with Essay Workbook

SAT II : Writing with Essay Workbook

SAT II : Writing with Essay Workbook

SAT II : Writing with Essay Workbook

SAT II : Writing with Essay Workbook

SAT II : Writing with Essay Workbook

SAT II : Writing with Essay Workbook

Answers

Answers

Part I

Chapter 1

✍ Identifying Prepositional Phrases

1. of New Jersey. 2. about a young girl and her dog. 3. every evening last week. 4. on the west coast. 5. between the age of 12 and 18. 6. in metal. 7. for 100 years. 8. of water. 9. into paper, pencils, and other various products. 10. on his arm.

✍ Prepositional Phrases

1. at the store, one of the U.S. Presidents. 2. at 99 miles per hour. 3. under her arm, with her other hand. 4. at thirty-seven degrees and a freezer at zero. 5. of the gauze pads on adhesive bandages, around wounds. 6. on a small farm in Korea in 1977. 7. During World War I, for submarines. 8. with human interaction with nature. 9. of Korea. 10. In 1492, for the spices of the Indies. 11. in front of school, in the morning. 12. their favorite snacks in spite of repeated warnings against eating too much fat. 13. regardless of my teachers' objections. 14. On a small island in the Pacific, of gold. 15. out of the soup.

Subject–Verb Agreement Exercise 1

1. are → is 2. were → was 3. correct 4. teacher were → teacher was 5. prove → proves 6. are → is 7. appear → appears 8. Here's → Here are 9. is → are 10. correct 11. correct 12. correct 13. ~ cathedral passes ~ → cathedral, more than fifty people pass each day. 14. correct 15. correct 16. is → are 17. is → are 18. correct 19. correct 20. are → is

Subject–Verb Agreement Exercise 2

1. was 2. were 3. presents 4. have 5. goes 6. sounds 7. plays 8. is 9. was 10. are

11. Three members of our team have made it to the championship tournament.

12. Many of my colleagues were excited because of the proposed raise.

13. Have any of the boys quit the team?

14. The batter, as well as the other players, was disappointed in the referee's decision.

15. All of the pineapples are rotten.

16. None of the classrooms were equipped with new computer monitors.

17. The boss, accompanied by three secretaries, leaves tomorrow on the business trip to Florida.

18. All but two of the chairs were broken.

19. Some of her plan has been approved.

20. Everyone does very well in school.

Subject–Verb Agreement Exercise 3

1. occlude 2. causes 3. are 4. forces 5. is 6. is 7. has 8. is 9. have 10. are

Subject–Verb Agreement Exercise 4

1. correct 2. is → are 3. correct 4. are → is 5. correct 6. correct 7. do → does 8. run → runs 9. have → had 10. were → was 11. correct 12. follow → follows 13. have → has 14. have → has 15. correct 16. correct 17. have → has 18. are → is 19. correct 20. holds → hold

Chapter 2

Pronoun Case Exercise 1

1. him 2. me 3. him 4. We 5. us 6. him 7. her 8. he 9. us 10. I 11. me 12. them 13. she 14. her 15. her 16. her 17. her 18. them 19. him 20. her 21. him 22. we 23. them, us 24. she 25. me 26. I 27. she 28. us 29. them 30. We 31. She 32. we 33. us 34. they 35. him 36. we 37. her, me 38. them 39. her 40. he

Pronoun Case Exercise 2

1. whom 2. who 3. whom 4. whom 5. whoever 6. whom 7. who 8. who 9. who 10. whom 11. Whom 12. who 13. our 14. who 15. me 16. me 17. them 18. him 19. whom 20. her

Pronoun Case Exercise 3

1. they 2. me 3. me 4. we 5. me 6. me 7. her 8. they 9. she 10. he
11. I → me 12. us → we 13. correct 14. myself → I 15. correct 16. correct 17. correct 18. her → she 19. correct 20. correct 21. who → whom 22. them → they 23. correct 24. us → our 25. correct 26. him → his 27. correct 28. him → his 29. himself → him 30. us → we

Chapter 3

Pronoun–Antecedent Agreement Exercise

1. their → his or her 2. their → his or her 3. their → his or her 4. their → his or her 5. correct 6. their → his 7. correct 8. All of the students enjoyed seeing Eiffel Tower. 9. their → her 10. their → his or her

1. Constant hallucinating frightened clarence.

2. Ray looked angry as he was bickering with John.

3. A sturdy friendship grew as Pastor Kim came to the house daily.

4. Raise the telescope to your eye, turning the telescope slowly to the right until it is focused.

5. Our job was to wash and remove the lebels from the old artifacts.

6. Being convinced of the importance of the committee's, President Gore ~

7. One of the passengers told the shuttle bus driver that the passenger had missed the stop.

8. Having enjoyed the author's writing style and surrealist plot I want to read her other books.

9. The treasurer became very nervous right after she recieved a report from the accountant.

10. The success of the rescue mission is due to a great deal of effort that went into planning the rescue mission, namely; hiring right sort of men and anticipating every emergency.

11. Considering the fact it would harm the economy, the Chinese were bitter at the United States for revoking its MFN status.

12. His partnership with Joe ended when Pyo drew the firm's money from the bank and flew to Korea.

13. Paul's thinking about EverQuest is his only interest.

14. In her vaudeville act Jeanie amused her audience by telling jokes, doing impersonations, and singing comic songs.

15. The teacher disapproved the boy's wearing roller blades to class.

16. The air conditioner's leak ran all over the living room floor.

17. Being extremely odd, she hides it from people she doesn't know well.

18. The epilogue implies that the hero died a martyr's death.

19. I consider photography an enjoyable hobby, so I take many pictures with my camera.

20. Domestic flights don't show any movies.

21. Although a virtuoso cellist, she never owned a valuable cello.

22. Tennis wouldn't cost me so much if I didn't hit so many balls over the fence.

23. Although well worth seeing, our guide said, it would take three hours.

24. Louis frequently wrote but none of his writings were ever published.

25. Being neighborly is important because you may need your neighbor's help someday in an emergency.

26. Some countries don't allow open feminist views.

27. Politicians have not met people's desire for honest public servants.

28. We didn't catch a single fish after having spent all day fly-fishing.

✐ Subject–Verb & Pronun Antecedent Agreement Exercise

1. takes 2. is 3. has 4. has 5. were 6. her 7. was 8. has 9. Is 10. Here are 11. his 12. is 13. is 14. doesn't 15. was 16. its 17. was 18. are 19. are 20. his 21. have → has 22. are → is 23. correct 24. correct 25. Are → Is 26. their → his or her 27. seem → seems 28. Is → Are 29. their → his 30. correct

Chapter 4

✐ Irregular Verbs: Past and Past Participle Forms

1. burst 2. began 3. beat 4. flown 5. broken 6. began 7. gone 8. do 9. chose 10. drew

11. chose → chosen 12. went → gone 13. correct 14. had froze → froze 15. fell → fallen 16. drew → drawn 17. correct 18. correct 19. bursted → burst 20. drank → drunk

21. rung 22. torn 23. spoken 24. saw 25. sprung 26. saw 27. ridden 28. ran 29. known 30. rung

31. ran → run 32. rang → rung 33. growed → grown 34. seen → sees
35. tore → torn 36. knew → known 37. took → taken 38. correct 39.
swum → swam 40. spoke → spoken

41. burst 42. froze 43. broken 44. flown 45. brew 46. fallen 47. began
48. known 49. correct 50. rung 51. driven 52. ridden 53. drank 54. ran
55. did 56. swum 57. came 58. stolen 59. chosen 60. sung 61. grown
62. spoken 63. gone 64. saw 65. gave

66. chose → chosen 67. bursted → burst 68. froze → frozen 69. went
→ gone 70. brung → brought

✍ Tense Exercise 1

1. Answers may vary

2. Answers may vary

3. Answers may vary

4. a 5. b 6. a 7. b 8. a

✍ Tense Exercise 2

1. previously studied → previously had studied 2. will receive → will have
receive 3. correct 4. correct 5. If she forgot → If she has forgot 6. she lived
→ she had lived 7. correct 8. If you told → If you had told 9. will be
teaching → will have taught 10. wound already → wound had already 11.
she performed → she had performed 12. would have → had 13. had been
cheating → had cheated 14. will be living → will have been living 15. you
started → you had started 16. would have read → had read 17. correct 18.
have been → be 19. manager has ordered → manager ordered 20. was not
→ had not been 21. Spending → Having spent 22. I did all → I had done
23. I already → I had already 24. rose → rises 25. have avoided → avoid

"Lie vs. Lay" Exercise

1. lay 2. laid 3. lying 4. lying 5. lying 6. lain 7. laid 8. lay 9. laid 10. laid 11. laying 12. lie 13. lain 14. lay 15. lay 16. laid 17. lain 18. was lying 19. laid 20. lies or lay

"Sit vs. Set" Exercise

1. sit 2. set 3. sat 4. sit 5. sat 6. setting 7. sat 8. sits 9. set 10. sitting

"Rise vs. Raise" Exercise

1. rises 2. raised 3. rising 4. rising 5. rising 6. rise 7. rising 8. raise 9. rose 10. rise

Confused Verbs Exercise

1. lies 2. raised 3. lie 4. lying 5. raised 6. rose 7. lie 8. set 9. lying 10. sit

Identifying Subjunctive Mood Exercise

1. I 2. S 3. S 4. S 5. I 6. I 7. I 8. S 9. I 10. S

Subjunctive Mood Exercise 1

1. was → were 2. was → were 3. correct 4. was → were 5. correct 6. was → were 7. was → were 8. was → were 9. correct 10. was → were

Subjunctive Mood Exercise 2

1. be 2. stop 3. come 4. were 5. were 6. forbid 7. prepare 8. was 9. Come 10. owned 11. were 12. pay 13. were 14. are

Verb Form and Tense Exercise

1. burst 2. lies 3. were 4. swam 5. had 6. Having cooked 7. had hoped 8. rise 9. had been hit 10. to have qualified 11. written 12. were 13. to pursue 14. Lay 15. won

1. correct 2. to have gone → to go 3. broke → has broken 4. you would have → you have 5. will be married → will have been married 6. was → were 7. lain → laid 8. already seen that movie? → have seen that movie already? 9. I never → I have never 10. took → had taken 11. correct 12. swum → swam 13. earthquakes were recorded → earthquakes had been recorded 14. laying → lying 15. If we would have → If we have, would not be stranded → would not had been stranded 16. have been → be 17. When the journalist ~, ~ batteries were going dead. 18. had forgotten → forgot 19. correct 20. supervisor, worked → supervisor, has worked

Chapter 5

Adj / Adv Exercise

1. correct 2. good → well 3. correct 4. correct 5. good → well 6. correct 7. good → well 8. well → good 9. correct 10. correct 11. correct 12. good → well 13. correct 14. good → well 15. correct 16. badly → bad 17. correct 18. correct 19. bad → badly 20. correct 21. good → well 22. correct 23. good → well 24. good → well 25. well → good

Comparison Exercise

1. correct 2. correct 3. best → better 4. correct 5. more clear → clearer 6. worser → worse 7. gracefuller → more graceful 8. darkest → darker 9. least → lesser 10. much more clearer → much clearer

Illogical Comparison Exercise

1. Joe is the worst batter in his whole team. 2. prettiest → prettier, 3. correct 4. correct 5. correct 6. correct 7. a better → the best 8. is faster → is the fastest 9. correct 10. correct 11. correct 12. to that master's → to master's 13. correct 14. correct 15. superior to you → superior than you 16. having

studied algebra → that I studied algebra 17. correct 18. less than Rome → less than that in Rome. 19. correct 20. the Greeks → the that of Greeks

Chapter 6

✐ Parallel Structure Exercise 1

1. correct 2. she has a body that is thin → a thin body 3. as fiction → as fictions 4. they deposit them → deposited 5. to force their → force to get their 6. its life lasts → for 7. correct 8. also interest → also with interest 9. cost → costly 10. than their → than to their 11. Ms. Moore. → Ms. Moore's. 12. because you can find one anywhere → availability 13. but that he dawdled → but dawdled 14. correct 15. correct 16. correct 17. correct 18. and foods that are starchy → and starchy foods. 19. both felt the → felt both the 20. both is the → is both the 21. correct 22. students. → students' 23. We feel certain that she is capable, she will succeed, and you will ~ → She is capable and will succeed that you will ~ 24. director → director's 25. she could be depended on → was dependable 26. as → that

✐ Parallel Structure Exercise 2

1. the well-behaved children and the delinquents are → the well-behaved and the delinquent children are 2. panaphobia is the name for the fear of everything. → the fear of everything is called panaphobia. 3. and to be cautions → cautiousness 4. ear plugs are worn by his family members. → his family members wear ear plugs.

5. stalks → stalked 6. is very strong → strength 7. the sweeping would be done by Regina, and the garbage would be taken out by Carley. → Regina would sweep, and Carley would take the garbage out. 8. to run, go skiing, and jogging. → to run, ski, and jog. 9. I washed the car, I dried off the car, and as for waxing it, I did that, too. → I washed, dried off and waxed the car. 10. but nothing was done by Josh. → but Josh did nothing. 11. you → he or she

12. He likes running and to go skiing and jogging. → He likes running, skiing, and jogging. 13. with the museum → with that in the museum 14. correct 15. and her sister → and to his sister 16. or your → or for your 17. but has strength → but strong

Chapter 7

Misplaced Modifiers Exercise

1. Haunted by memory of the men who had died unrecognized in the black ops, the navy seal commander was honored for his valor.

2. The castle moat has a drawbridge, which can only be manipulated by the drawbridge-raiser, to permit the passage of people and cargo.

3. In his anthropology class, Indiana Jones described his archeological finds from the jungle.

4. In Miami, Florida, there have been many meetings held to make arrangements for Elian Gonzalez's returning to Cuba.

5. The company now runs a full time daycare center for any employee who has children.

6. Through binoculars, our recon scout sighted a figure, which she could not identify.

7. A high-tech microwave, which I bought for the office kitchen, gave everyone a great deal of pleasure.

8. Miss Rogers, who later became Mrs. Datsun, donated 2 million dollars to fund the dormitory.

9. The president discussed with members of the congress the possibility of filling every pothole in the United States.

10. Father bought a new radio, which was supposed to make soothing sounds at night to promote sleep, from a fast-talking salesclerk.

Dangling Modifiers Exercise

1. Left alone in the house, he was terrified by the thunderstorm.

2. The lawyers evidence for the defendant was strong.

3. Our practice session were lengthened to win the tournament this year.

4. As she run up the wet stairs, her foot slipped on the step.

5. Aluminum foil is more effective for keeping food fresh than saran wrap.

6. Avoid any cars when crossing the street.

7. Tampers began to flare while joking mockingly with friends.

8. After flying in mist for two hours, the pilot was about to see better as the thick clouds began to disperse.

9. The bystanders all stopped to marvel at the enormous and visually striking statue.

10. I had little strength left for the evening outing after working in the office all day.

Dangling & Misplaced Modifiers Exercise

1. A bell must be rung before gaining admittance to his apartment.

2. I saw a man stumbling blindly in the fog.

3. Critics considered the performance, which had run for many weeks, a success.

4. In oreder to successfully market a product, its design must be user-friendly as well as aesthetically pleasing to customers.

5. After helping the old man cross the street, I had no event through the rest of the walk.

6. All aspects of the motion must be argued carefully in order to win the approval of the judge.

7. The jokes have to be twice as good in order to win over a hostile audience.

8. The lockers, which stand in the hallway, are on constant watch by the monitor.

9. The train must be on time to reach my office by 8:15.

10. Did you hear the news on the radio about the explosions on the ship?

11. A feeling of frustration is no surprise to be stuck in traffic for hours.

12. He went to the old church on Cemetery Hill, to pray for the people.

13. If used only natural ingredients, a healthy dinner is certain.

14. In his entire family, only his wife loved him.

15. He lowered the volume when he picked up the phone.

✐ More Dangling & Misplaced Modifiers Exercise

1. Flying at an altitude of several thousand feet, one can see the breadth of an entire state.

2. Living constantly under the eyes of a prison guard, he had increasing anxiety that made him insane.

3. The principal with his signature gave a detention notice to one of the students.

4. Plans for a new gymnasium to replace the abandoned football field have finally been approved after four years of bickering.

5. On the way to our grandmother's house, we saw a pack of wild wolves.

6. A great deal of persistence is key to succeed in anything.

7. Before the contest began, Cameron wanted to know what the referee had said to the two captains.

8. This bank approves loans of any size to individuals with good credit history.

9. The smoke alarm went off while trying to prepare dinner.

10. The museum's curator showed a tropical insect that had curious markings I have never seen before to me.

Chapter 8

✐ Sentence Revision Exercise

1. Although walking takes longer than running, it is better for your joins.

2. With no anxieties about my future plans, I was having a great time at the party.

3. We tried both persuasion and bribery at the bouncer to get into the exclusive club.

4. If you leave at ten o'clock, you can arrive in time to catch the plane.

5. Going to toy stores and roller-skating were childhood treats.

6. No protest should be registered if you are hit accidentally by a ball.

7. Jose had been appointed president not only of the company but of the softball team.

8. Through the window, he saw Lester working out.

9. Gill didn't know whether to put the dishwashing liquid in before turning on the water or to do it in the reverse order.

10. Sometimes, she goes to school poorly groomed, wearing dirty jeans, and with out brushed hair.

Run-on Sentences Exercise

1. First try to do these grammar problems by yourself. However, if you can't do it, don't look at your friend's book. You can ask the teacher for help.

2. We have a pet cat; it always scratches the furniture and sheds hair all over the place.

3. A suggestion box has been placed in the hall just outside the supervisor's office. By this means, employees can express their complaints about the company anonymously.

4. A new committee is being formed for the study of social delinquency. In the committee, psychiatrists will create solutions instead of just identifying problems.

5. Eddie took an art elective and discovered he had talent; now he spends his afternoons at the art academy to improve his technique.

6. life, at $\rightarrow$ life; at 7. next, mp3s $\rightarrow$ next; mp3s 8. America, these $\rightarrow$ America; these 9. creatures, they are $\rightarrow$ creatures, for instance they are 10. system, so far $\rightarrow$ system. So far

Fragments & Run-ons Exercise

1. Gary; who → Gary, who / deadline, he → deadline; furthermore, he 2. once. When → once, when / desperate, I hadn't → desperate, because I hadn't 3. lessons, academics → lessons, because academics 4. move; almost → move, almost 5. Russo. Where → Russo; where

6. Because wild rumors had been circulating, everyone was asking questions about the new kid, Daniel La Russo; where he was from and what he was wearing.

7. After reading Anne McCaffrey's fantasy novel, which uses strong narrative styles and vast imagination, I learned to like it.

8. I have learned to recognize several kinds of people, especially the kind that gets pleasure out of being mean. When I see one of these coming, I run for cover.

9. During the Victorian period, when girls were considered frail flowers to be kept safe and separate, women's colleges were first established in America.

10. correct

Chapter 9

Idioms Exercise

1. with 2. from 3. in 4. in 5. on 6. upon 7. to 8. to 9. about 10. in 11. of or to 12. in 13. with 14. on 15. for 16. in or at 17. to 18. with 19. from 20. to

Double Negatives Exercise

1. theory, scarcely no → theory, no 2. has never been → has been 3. without hardly any → without any 4. for scarcely → for 5. without → with 6. hardly no → no 7. be scarcely → be 8. hardly any commentators have criticized it. → no commentators have criticized it yet. 9. is not an → is an 10. barely nothing → nothing

Part II

Confused Words List 1

1. you're, lie 2. accepted, into 3. advise, advice 4. effect 5. all together 6. than 7. Whose 8. stationary 9. raise, rises 10. dessert 11. lose 12. its 13. principle 14. already 15. though

1. correct 2. correct 3. were → where 4. too → to 5. correct 6. then → than 7. correct 8. correct 9. Who's → Whose 10. correct 11. correct 12. Its → It's 13. it's → its 14. correct 15. their → there

Confused Words List 2

1. conscience 2. personal 3. allusions 4. compliment 5. latter 6. capital 7. built 8. elude 9. breathe 10. cite 11. choose 12. morale 13. descent 14. counsel 15. farther

1. capital → capitol 2. morale → moral 3. site → sight 4. correct 5. latter → later 6. correct 7. personnel → personal 8. compliments → complements 9. consul → counsel 10. correct 11. breadth → breath 12. correct 13. site → cite 14. correct 15. correct

Confused Words List 3

🖉 Exercise 1

1. illicit 2. eminent 3. prophecy 4. canvas 5. confident 6. carat 7. averse 8. exceed 9. clique 10. emigrated 11. disperse 12. discomfort 13. epitaph 14. expend 15. forte

🖉 Exercise 2

1. adopted → adapted 2. incidence → incident 3. eminent → imminent 4. canvas → canvass 5. formally → formerly 6. correct 7. correct 8. correct 9. adverse → averse 10. correct 11. correct 12. correct 13. forte → fort 14. correct 15. correct

Confused Words List 4

🖉 Exercise 1

1. among 2. alumna 3. advantage 4. bad 5. number 6. annoy 7. anxious 8. annual 9. surprised 10. always 11. Because 12. abbreviate 13. a lot 14. alternate 15. about

🖉 Exercise 2

1. "are I not" → "am I not" 2. alright → all right 3. correct 4. as good as → so good as 5. correct 6. correct 7. as → like 8. correct 9. correct 10. correct 11. correct 12. correct 13. correct 14. correct 15. as → because

Confused Words List 5

1. bunch 2. from 3. take 4. that 5. enthusiastic 6. expect 7. disinterested 8. May 9. constantly 10. are 11. have 12. Because of 13. one another 14. Every one 15. just as good

1. correct 2. correct 3. correct 4. correct 5. on account of → because of 6. I dislike all insects, such as ants, cockroaches, and flies. 7. correct 8. correct 9. bunch → group 10. equally as good → just as good 11. each other → one another 12. correct 13. correct 14. correct 15. correct

Confused Words List 6

1. fewer 2. Human beings 3. former, latter 4. Much 5. habit 6. infer 7. as if 8. in regard to 9. regardless 10. hanged 11. graduate from 12. healthful 13. good 14. lend 15. flout

1. guess → think or suppose 2. finalized → completed 3. where → in which 4. correct 5. kind of → somewhat 6. is when → occurs when 7. were → was 8. was → were 9. correct 10. hisself → himself 11. Much → Many 12. correct 13. is when → occurs when 14. correct 15. Humans → Human beings

Confused Words List 7

1. because of 2. to 3. I 4. are 5. pleasant 6. that 7. have 8. refer 9. oral 10. to 11. off 12. manages 13. respectively 14. stop 15. satisfactory

1. correct 2. performance again. → performance. 3. correct 4. the same as → in the same way as 5. correct 6. refer back to → refer 7. correct 8. because → that 9. over → to 10. nice → kind 11. correct 12. referred back → referred 13. myself again. → myself. 14. run → manage 15. on account of → because of

Confused Words List 8

1. condition 2. have 3. some time 4. testimony 5. to 6. who 7. whereas 8. am 9. whom 10. have 11. Whoever 12. had 13. themselves 14. sometimes 15. invaluable

1. while → whereas 2. sink down → sink 3. correct 4. correct 5. Whom → Who 6. and → to 7. correct 8. invaluable → valuable 9. correct 10. who → which 11. correct 12. correct 13. correct 14. correct

공저자 소개

• 표기훈

전 Jaon Academy (New Jersey, USA) SAT I , SAT II , TOEFL 강의

전 English and Math Institute (New Jersey, USA) SAT I , SAT II , TOEFL 강의

전 Achieve Academy (New Jersey, USA) SAT I , SAT II , TOEFL 강의

현재 SAT I , SAT II , TOEFL 강의 (서울 강남 대치동)

• 이지선

Columbia University (New York, USA) 영문과 졸업

Columbia Law School (New York, USA)

전 Jaon Academy (New Jersey, USA) SAT I , SAT II 강의

현재 Achieve Academy (New Jersey, USA) SAT II 강의

SAT II :
Writing with Essay Workbook
– 미국에서 배우는 영어 문법과 작문 –

2003년 5월 15일 인쇄
2003년 5월 20일 발행

지은이 / 표 기 훈 · 이 지 선

발행인 / 김 영 철

발행처 / 학 문 사 HMP

서울특별시 종로구 사직동 7-2번지 사학회관

☎ (대) (02)738-5118 FAX 733-8998

(대구지사) (053)422-5000~3 FAX 424-7111

(부산지사) (051)502-8104 FAX 503-8121

등록번호 제1-1883호

가 격 20,000원

© HAKMUN PUBLISHING CO. 2003
ISBN 89 – 467 – 8214 – 5
E-mail: hakmun@hakmun.co.kr
http:/www.hakmun.co.kr

Printed in Korea